U. S. IMPORT QUOTAS: COSTS AND CONSEQUENCES

U. S. IMPORT QUOTAS: COSTS AND CONSEQUENCES

Ilse Mintz

American Enterprise Institute for Public Policy Research
Washington, D. C.

Ilse Mintz, retired professor of economics, Columbia University, is senior staff member, National Bureau of Economic Research.

ISBN 0-8447-3095-5

Domestic Affairs Study 10, February 1973

Library of Congress Catalog Card No. L. C. 73-76159

Printed in the United States of America

PREFATORY NOTE

I am grateful to Professor Gottfried Haberler of the American Enterprise Institute who read a draft of this study and made many helpful suggestions. I also had the benefit of an informative discussion with Mrs. Helen Junz, Miss Betty Barker and Mr. Daniel Roxon of the Federal Reserve Board. Further, I am indebted to Mr. Fred Bergsten of the Brookings Institution for advice on sources of information. Last but not least, my thanks are due to officials of a number of government agencies who gave most generously of their valuable time to furnish me information and data. Needless to say, I am solely responsible for the views expressed in this paper.

The text of this study was completed in March 1972.

CONTENTS

1
INTRODUCTION AND SUMMARY

The Rising Importance of Import Quotas

United States foreign trade policy, like that of most other countries, faces in opposite directions. On the one hand, it stands for trade liberalization and in fact, under the Trade Agreements Act and its extensions, tariffs have been reduced substantially. On the other hand, policy is guided by a "no injury philosophy."[1] As soon as the lowering of tariffs or other circumstances lead to a more than negligible rise in imports and thus could begin to have the beneficial effect of pushing resources from inefficient to efficient uses, the policy is reversed and measures are taken to prevent such "disruption."

This posture is reflected in the U.S. trade policy of the fifties and sixties. While tariffs have been reduced in successive steps culminating in the Kennedy Round, the use of nontariff barriers has increased and continues to increase rapidly. How is this possible since such controls not only have been prohibited specifically by the General Agreement on Tariffs and Trade (GATT), but also have been consistently opposed by the United States? It is possible because a new protectionist device has been invented, a device which gets around all international prohibitions and domestic inhibitions and which is compatible with an official posture of unalterable opposition to quotas.

This new tool is the "voluntary" quota, imposed by exporters or an exporting nation on its sales of certain commodities. Since it is

---

[1] Cf. Mordechai E. Kreinin, *International Economics* (New York: Harcourt Brace, 1971), pp. 270, 271. Also, Ingo Walter, "Nontariff Barriers and the Export Performance of Developing Economies," *American Economic Review*, May 1971. p. 195.

the exporter who "wishes" to limit his exports, such quotas are regarded as an entirely different species of control than the ones proscribed by GATT and rejected by the U.S. government. After all, so the reasoning goes, international regulation cannot prescribe to an exporter how much he is to sell and the fact that he informs the importing country of his intentions does not make this country guilty of trade restrictions. Thus liberal consciences are assuaged while a particularly harmful form of restriction is spreading. That the exporter's restrictions are imposed under the threat that the importer will otherwise use compulsion and that the "voluntary" character is a myth does not seem to matter.

The shift in the U.S. attitude toward trade restriction is part of a worldwide trend. In the early years after World War II it was the basic philosophy of the Bretton Woods system that quotas should not be used as a means of regulating international trade, and this principle underlies some of the fundamental rules of GATT.[2] Although these rules allow for many exceptions, they helped in the step-by-step reduction of the use of direct controls which had been built up, first in the depression of the 1930s, then during the war and the so-called dollar shortage thereafter.

The GATT rules were an attempt to prevent repetition of the disastrous effects on economic activity and international goodwill that had resulted from the trade barriers of the 1930s. GATT became so successful in its fight for abolition of controls that it published, in 1959 and 1960, "liberalization communiques" which announced proudly that one or another country had removed restrictions on imports.[3] The greater freedom helped to bring about a record expansion of international trade which enriched the world.

The present, changed attitude is reflected in the proposed Foreign Trade and Investment Act, widely known as the Burke-Hartke bill.[4]

---

[2] "No prohibitions and restrictions other than duties, taxes or other charges, whether made effective through quotas, import or export licenses or other measures, shall be instituted or maintained by any contracting party on the importation of any product of the territory of any other contracting party or on the exportation or sale for export of any product destined for the territory of any contracting party." *General Agreement on Tariffs and Trade*, Geneva, 1947, Article XI.

See also Robert E. Baldwin, *Nontariff Distortions of International Trade*, The Brookings Institution, Washington, D. C., 1970, p. 175.

[3] Gerard Curzon, *Multilateral Commercial Diplomacy* (London: Michael Joseph, 1965), p. 155.

[4] Introduced in the 92nd Congress in September 1971 by Representative James A. Burke, D.-Mass., and Senator Vance Hartke, D.-Ind., and subsequently reintroduced in the 93rd Congress (as H.R. 62 and S. 151).

If enacted, this bill would place virtually all U.S. imports under quotas, excepting only imports of goods not produced domestically. All covered imports would be limited to the average import level of 1965-69. The result would be a very large cutback in imports. The bill has considerable support in Congress, in the general public, and particularly in sectors of organized labor.

It is not surprising that those who stand to gain directly from protection will fight for it. But it is also understandable that many other well-meaning people join them in the belief that most imports are harmful to the national economy.

Plan of Study

Clearly, it is important to obtain as much information as possible on this kind of economic policy. This is the purpose of the present study. Although it was written before the new bill was submitted to the Congress, the study is relevant to an evaluation of the bill's provisions, because it analyzes the impact of the import quotas currently in force and thus provides a basis for judging the proposed expansion of such quotas.

Until recently import quotas have received much less attention in the literature than tariffs.[5] This is understandable in view of the complex and often obscure nature of such quotas, details of which are often not published. The difficulty in obtaining information deters investigators from making the careful study of quotas that they deserve. This lack of attention applies especially to the relatively new tool of "voluntary" quotas, which in fact is either not mentioned at all in current texts or given cursory treatment only.

The many ways in which quotas differ from tariffs will be analyzed in chapter 2. This comparison should throw light on both the causes and the effects of the current preference for quotas. The complex problems of measuring the costs of quotas are explored in chapter 3. The costs of sugar and textile quotas are estimated in chapters 4 and 5 and the final chapter gives brief descriptions of quotas on dairy products, oil, meat, steel and other commodities.

Since this study is confined to United States quotas, features of foreign quotas, which are not pertinent also to U.S. quotas, are not discussed. Of course, this does not imply that foreign quotas are less harmful to the countries which impose them than domestic quotas are to the United States.

---

[5] A recent study of quotas is Robert E. Baldwin, *Nontariff Distortions*. A good, brief survey is C. Fred Bergsten, *The Cost of Import Restrictions to American Consumers* (New York: American Importers Association, 1972).

Protectionism: For and Against

The most important protectionist argument is the cheap-labor or low-wage argument. The question is always asked: How can U.S. industry compete with the industry of countries where wages are only a fraction of U.S. wages? To many people and organizations the obvious answer is a call for protection to overcome the wage differential. However, high U.S. wages clearly reflect high U.S. productivity. This fact can best be demonstrated by recalling that the United States, where wages since colonial days have been generally higher than in the rest of the world, nevertheless has sold more abroad than it bought in 92 of the last 96 years (from 1876 through 1971).

But in certain industries, it will be replied, the difference in productivity is not sufficient to offset the difference in wages. While this is true, it merely points to the fact that the productivity of certain industries is substantially *below average*. If average wages in the U.S. are, say, three times as high as those abroad, average U.S. productivity must be about three times as high as foreign productivity. But of course this average ratio does not prevail in every industry and with respect to every product.

Industries suffering from import competition are typically those whose productivity is below average and which pay the lowest wages, whereas the opposite is typically true of export industries. What the protectionist argument in fact suggests is that as much labor and capital as possible be kept in industries with low wages and productivity instead of letting such industries contract in favor of those where both factors are high even by U.S. standards. But just as the production of wheat on the eastern seaboard had to give way to production in the midwestern plains, so production of certain goods should be reduced or discontinued when acquiring them abroad in exchange for exports is more economical.

This argument should not be construed to imply criticism of any import-competing industry. Just as the New England farmer was not any less efficient than the farmer in the Dakotas, so the weak industry may be perfectly modern and efficient in using available resources. The "inefficiency" lies in the nature of an industry that requires relatively large amounts of relatively expensive resources to turn out a product procured more cheaply elsewhere.

Another protectionist argument is—for good reasons—rarely stated explicitly, but may be more influential than any other. Its gist is that changes in relative international costs should not be permitted to cause shifts from one industry to another because such shifts are too painful for those involved. This argument disregards the continuous rapid changes which characterize the American economy. How incredibly mobile this economy is can be seen, for instance, from the fact that in manufacturing alone almost 11 million job changes and new hires occurred in a recent year.[6] The vast majority of shifts is not due to imports, of course, but to changes in technology, in consumers' tastes, and—mainly—in government policies (such as the recent decline in the aerospace industry). These shifts are accepted because it is generally understood that a dynamic economy must adapt to change and that inability to transform means economic stagnation. Why should an exception be made for industries hurt by imports?

A third protectionist argument, particularly impressive in a time of high unemployment, is that rising imports reduce the number of jobs available to American workers. The effect of imports on employment seems too obvious to be questioned. And yet, a quick look at the data should raise doubts, since it is by no means usual for falling imports to be accompanied by rising employment. The argument is, indeed, fallacious because it ignores the fact that the government would create sufficient demand for a reduction of unemployment were it not for the fear of increasing inflation. But when domestic purchasing power is absorbed by rising imports it can be replaced without danger of inflationary effects. The total demand for domestic goods thus should not be reduced by the growth of imports. Put another way, reduction of imports requires reduction of total domestic demand if it is not to be inflationary.

Also, this protectionist argument overlooks the connection between exports and imports. After a while, a rise in imports will cause an approximately equal rise in exports, for the number of workers required to produce an extra dollar's worth of exports is only negligibly smaller than the number set free by an extra dollar's worth of imports.[7] Temporary unemployment will, of course, arise here as with any other change in the economy, but its volume and duration can be lessened by the adjustment assistance that is discussed below.

Nor are the interests of labor served by freezing jobs in the industries competing with imports. These jobs typically pay less well than do jobs in export industries, even if wages in the former were high compared to foreign ones. "For example, a weighted index of wage rates for production workers in manufacturing whose jobs depended on exports in 1966, the latest year for which information is

---

[6] Council of Economic Advisers, *Annual Report*, 1970, p. 151.

[7] Mordechai E. Kreinin, *Alternative Commercial Policies—Their Effect on the American Economy* (Michigan State University, 1967), p. 132.

available, was 8 percent higher than the average earnings in jobs which might have been created by import replacement."[8]

A fourth protectionist argument, which appears especially appealing in 1972, claims that the U.S. balance of payments deficit could be reduced by import controls. Again the argument overlooks the repercussions of import restrictions. These are likely to appear in several ways. Less developed countries whose sales in the U.S. are cut will simply have fewer dollars to spend on U.S. goods. These and other foreign countries may also retaliate by taking similar measures against U.S. goods.

Domestically, the money not spent by Americans on imports will, for the most part, be diverted to other goods, thereby driving up their prices and encouraging imports while curtailing exports. Due to these repercussions, attempts to improve the balance of payments for more than a few months through increased protection have usually failed.

Moreover, exports suffer from import reduction even without retaliation. Many imported goods are used in producing export goods so that when the prices of imports are raised through protection exports too become more expensive and less competitive. This result is well illustrated in our later analysis of steel quotas.

Protective Import Quotas

Among protective devices import quotas are by far the most effective and, hence, the most dangerous, as will be argued in the next chapter. One of their particularly harmful aspects is the unpredictability of the price rises they set in motion. When raising tariff rates the government knows the upper limit to which the price of the protected good may rise, but with quantitative restrictions there is no such limit.

The allocation of quotas is another troublesome aspect. The profitable rights to import must somehow be assigned either through a government agency or an industrial cartel. The dangers of having public or private officials decide who is to get what share of a valuable privilege is obvious.[9] In addition, the machinery and red tape needed to assign and control the quotas are costly for government and business alike.

A further disadvantage of quotas as compared with tariffs is their effect on income distribution. The revenue from a tariff is received

---

[8] Council of Economic Advisers, *Annual Report*, 1971, p. 157.

[9] Kenneth W. Dam shows very well, in the case of oil quotas, how the power to allocate profits is used for purposes which have nothing to do with protection. See *Implementation of Import Quotas: The Case of Oil* (Washington: The Brookings Institution, 1971).

by the government and thus by the public at large. Quota profits, on the other hand, go to those who hold the rights to import under the quotas. The windfall may go to the foreign exporters or the domestic importers. (It is possible to auction off the quotas in order to channel this profit to the government, but this method has never been applied in the U.S.)

The U.S. uses both mandatory and "voluntary" quotas. The latter—a relatively new device—are limitations accepted by exporters on their own sales in order to prevent the U.S. government from imposing mandatory quotas on the goods in question. These "voluntary" quotas are even more dangerous and more costly (other things being equal) than mandatory ones because they circumvent international agreements which prohibit quantitative restrictions. They are dangerous also because they lead the public to believe mistakenly that such arrangements are mainly the foreigners' concern and of little consequence for the United States.

Adjustment Assistance

Import restriction is not the only possible policy for aiding an industry which suffers from growing foreign competition. A much less expensive and more efficient approach is to facilitate the adjustments that injured firms and workers must make.

Since all citizens share the benefits of a liberal trade policy, its costs should not be a burden for a few. This principle is recognized by the adjustment assistance provisions of the Trade Expansion Act of 1962. These provisions enable the government to assist through grants and loans the transfer of resources into more productive and competitive branches of industry. The assistance takes the form of programs for relocating and retraining workers and extending financial help to business firms so that they can shift into more competitive production lines. The aim is to shift resources *out* of the industry instead of *into* it.

Use of such assistance "expanded notably during 1970. For the first time since the program's inception, the President authorized firms and workers in three industries to apply directly to the secretaries of the Departments of Commerce and Labor for assistance. The number of workers and firms actually certified for assistance, including some in other industries that had requested assistance individually from the Tariff Commission, increased greatly during 1970."[10] Further expansion of the program is planned for fiscal 1972.

---

[10] Council of Economic Advisers, *Annual Report*, 1971, p. 156.

Authority for loans of $100 million and additional loan guarantees of the same amount are requested. If actually delivered, financial assistance in these amounts would constitute a several-fold increase in the quantity of similar aid that will be extended to firms in the current fiscal year. To supplement this assistance to firms, the number of workers paid training and relocation benefits is projected to increase some 55 percent in fiscal 1972.[11]

It would be desirable to broaden the program even more so that assistance could be offered to entire communities injured by import competition to help them diversify their industrial base. One important point in favor of this policy is financial. The costs of adjustment assistance are by their very nature transitory. They must decline and finally vanish as the transfer of labor and other resources is effected. On the other hand, the costs of a quota continue as long as the quota is in effect. It is quite misleading, therefore, to compare (as has been done occasionally) the annual costs of quotas, which can continue almost indefinitely, to the once-for-all investment in efficiency which the adjustment assistance represents.

Needless to say, adjustment assistance is not costless. It is the price paid to an injured minority by a majority which benefits from the greater efficiency of the economy. Some argue, nevertheless, that in the case of large industries this price would be too high. Thus Stanley Nehmer, deputy assistant secretary of commerce, believes that such assistance to the textile industry "would bring us to the threshold of a major financial undertaking that staggers the imagination."[12] However, this argument disregards the fact that the cost of *not* adjusting is as much a function of the size of the industry as is the cost of adjusting. What matters is how many dollars of future costs can be saved by each dollar invested in adjustment assistance. "Invested" is the correct term here because, to repeat, the cost of transition is a one-time outlay in contrast to the long-term or even indefinite cost of protection by import quotas.

Quota Costs Summarized

The present paper presents a rough estimate of the costs of certain import quotas, both mandatory and "voluntary." These costs are both

---

[11] U.S. Congress, Joint Economic Committee, *1971 Joint Economic Report*, p. 6.
[12] Stanley Nehmer, "Remarks Prepared for Delivery at the Board Meeting of the National Association of Wool Manufacturers," Washington, D. C., November 18, 1970, p. 11.

direct and indirect (so-called "dynamic" costs). The latter result from the impairment of competition and the consequent decline in efficiency and technological progress that are caused by the quantitative restrictions. These costs, though perhaps larger than the direct ones, had to be excluded from this study in the absence of available estimates. The preparation of such estimates would represent a large and difficult undertaking quite beyond the limited scope of this paper.

Even the direct costs of quotas have been calculated only in a few instances because of the difficulties involved. The direct costs may be defined as those incurred in producing goods at home by prevailing methods instead of importing them at lower costs. Among these direct quota costs the following four types should be distinguished.

First, there are "production costs," namely, the difference between the costs of the domestic, import-replacing output and the costs of the foregone imports. Production costs measure the waste in U.S. resources. Secondly, there are "consumption costs," namely, the loss suffered by consumers from being obliged to switch their purchases to less desirable substitutes because of the scarcity of the goods limited by quotas. These two types of costs are both a dead loss to the national economy.

The third type of costs, "import costs," arises from the raised prices of whatever imports are still admitted after the quota is imposed. Import costs are also national costs whenever the exporters control the right to sell and thus obtain the quota profit. This is of necessity true of all "voluntary" quotas and also of some mandatory ones. When U.S. importers hold quota rights and thus receive the profits, however, import costs are not part of national costs but constitute transfer costs, representing a gain for U.S. importers at the expense of U.S. consumers.

The fourth type of quota costs is always in the nature of "transfer costs," for it represents the consumers' additional expenditures on such domestic output as would have been produced at home at lower prices without the existing quota. There is a transfer of income from consumer to producer.

The sum of the national cost (the first three) and the transfer cost is the total user cost of the quota. The total user cost is not as difficult to measure as the national cost is and, as a result, there are a few more estimates of the former than of the latter. Even this larger number does not suffice, however, for presenting the aggregate cost of all existing U.S. quotas.

Two estimates of national costs can be cited here. One estimate, from the literature, is for oil quotas which are found to cost the nation

$1,500 million to $2,000 million a year. The second estimate of national costs was prepared for this study and refers to sugar quotas, whose indicated costs come to around $400 million a year, or as much as 20 to 25 percent of the retail value of U.S. sugar consumption. If these percentages are at all typical, they show that the nation's loss from quotas equals a very sizable part of the value of the products concerned.

Total costs generally are much higher because they also include the transfer cost, as defined. Those of oil quotas, for instance, are estimated at about $5,000 million or 40 percent of the annual value of oil production at home. The total user cost of U.S. sugar quotas is figured in this study at 32 percent to 39 percent of the total U.S. expenditure on sugar, or $580 to $700 million a year.

The total annual cost of textile quotas (all fibers) amounts to $2,500 million to $4,800 million, as estimated in chapter 5. This estimate is based on the cautious assumption that import quotas raise textile prices by a mere 5 to 10 percent. Regarding meat quotas, the total user cost has been estimated at $600 million annually.

No matter how rough these figures are, they indicate clearly that quotas impose a heavy burden on consumers. Moreover, the burden weighs most heavily on those with low incomes because the prohibited imports consist, in many instances, of inexpensive goods, such as the cheaper cuts of meat and low-price textiles. A sales tax on such goods, of equal impact on income, would be considered intolerable—and so would import quotas if the public understood their effect.

2
QUOTAS VERSUS TARIFFS

Imports can be reduced to any desired level, including complete elimination, by either quotas or tariffs. An increase in the home production of the protected good, along with an increase in its price and a fall in its consumption will occur whether a tariff or a quota is imposed. They are both protectionist instruments.[1]

The common effects of protectionist policies, as opposed to free trade, will not be discussed here. The purpose of this chapter is the more limited one of bringing out the differences between the two protectionist tools. It is assumed throughout that the import of some commodity is to be reduced to a certain level and the question then arises over the relative merit of the two tools in bringing about this reduction.[2]

Traditionally, the term "import quotas" refers to mandatory quotas, i.e., quantitative limits fixed by the importing country's government. In the last 15 years or so, however, more and more use has

---

[1] Bhagwati has recently shown that exactly "equivalent" effects of the two commercial policies occur only when markets are competitive. With the introduction of monopoly this equivalence breaks down. Bhagwati's discovery has led to an extended discussion in the scientific journals and to appropriate modification of the theory. See Jagdish Bhagwati, "On the Equivalence of Tariffs and Quotas," in Baldwin et al., eds., *Trade, Growth, and the Balance of Payments*, Essays in Honor of Gottfried Haberler (Chicago: Rand McNally & Company, 1965), pp. 53-67. For other contributions see, for instance, W. M. Corden, *The Theory of Protection* (Oxford, England: Clarendon Press, 1971), pp. 212-15; and articles by Mordechai E. Kreinin and Ingo Walter in *Kyklos*, 1970, pp. 75-78, and 1971, p. 111. The comparisons between tariffs and quotas in this paper, however, are not concerned with the issues raised in the equivalence discussion.

[2] The discussion of this section was greatly aided by Gottfried Haberler's pioneer work on the subject, *Quantitative Trade Controls, Their Causes and Nature* (League of Nations, 1943), ch. 4.

been made of a newer device, the so-called "voluntary" quota. These quotas are fixed by the exporting industry and/or its government, usually in agreement with the government of the importing country. The following discussion will include mandatory as well as "voluntary" quotas. Differences between the two will be pointed out in the last section of this chapter.

In limiting the discussion to quotas and tariffs we are neglecting a third possibility which deserves at least a passing mention: subsidies paid by government to the protected industry. To be effective, these subsidies must be sufficient to keep the industry going despite the low prices forced on it by foreign competition. Subsidies have two great advantages over tariffs and direct controls. First, consumption patterns are not distorted by raised prices; and, second, the cost of maintaining the industry, which must be borne by the taxpayers, is known and hence open to public debate.

It is precisely for this second reason that subsidies are unpopular and rarely used. Nevertheless, awareness of this policy alternative is important. Throughout the following discussion it should be kept in mind that tariffs and quotas are not the only choices open to policy makers whose aim is the protection of an industry.

Subsidies and tariffs have one important element in common: they work through the price system. They reduce imports indirectly, either by reducing the price of domestic substitutes or by increasing the price of the imported good. By contrast, import quotas determine directly and precisely the maximum amount of a good, measured in physical units or in value, which is admitted to a country in a given period of time. Once the indicated amount has been imported, the quota is "filled" and further importation is prohibited until the next quota period. It is this simplicity of direct controls which explains much of their popularity.

Flexibility

One advantage commonly attributed to quotas over tariffs is that the first are administratively more flexible, i.e., more easily imposed and more easily removed than import duties. In most instances it is difficult to raise tariff rates. It requires legislative action that is time consuming and that may be prevented or delayed by commercial agreements or by the rules of GATT. Introducing a quota, on the contrary, is relatively easy. Even mandatory quotas require, in some instances, only an administrative decision under an existing law, thus avoiding the hurdles of congressional procedures. Voluntary quotas are even more flexible, for they can be agreed upon at any time without formal procedures or legislation. This aspect of voluntary quotas is well illustrated by the U.S. steel quota which has made it possible to reduce steel imports in the face of the prohibition against raising the steel tariff. One must note in addition that the superior flexibility of voluntary limitation is due to the omission of full public debate and the absence of proper representation of the public interest.

Flexibility also refers to the supposed tolerance by foreign countries of quotas, and especially of "voluntary" ones. Because quotas are regarded as temporary measures—in contrast to tariffs which are deemed to be more or less permanent—they are not expected to evoke retaliation. But it is hard to tell whether this belief is always justified. In some cases quotas evoked grave protests and also official retaliatory action against American goods.[3] In other instances retaliation may consist in the tightening of the foreign countries' quotas and thus be less visible but not necessarily less effective than retaliation through the raising of foreign duties. (It is possible also that foreign suppliers accept quotas because they gain more from higher prices than they lose from smaller volume; but this point has nothing to do with flexibility.)

Flexibility is supposed to mean not only that quotas are more easily imposed than tariffs, but also that they are more easily removed. If true, this would be a merit even from the anti-quota point of view. But whether this claim is justified is difficult to tell. Certainly, most quotas imposed before and during World War II by developed nations were lifted in the 1950s; but the same years also saw a considerable lowering of tariffs, and I know of no attempt to determine which kind of liberalization was "easier" or more frequent.[4]

Thus the claim that quotas are more flexible than tariffs is justified in the sense that it is usually easier to impose a quota than to raise a tariff duty. This superior flexibility is without merit, of course, if expansion of trade is considered desirable. It is hardly reasonable to make a great effort in order to prevent tariffs from interfering with international trade and then praise a rival method for such interference.

[3] Cf., for instance, Delbert A. Snider, *Introduction to International Economics* (Homewood, Illinois: Richard D. Irwin, Inc., 1971), p. 201.

[4] Of the nine articles on which quotas were imposed under the Agricultural Adjustment Act of 1935, only four are subject to quotas currently. See United States Tariff Commission, *Quantitative Import Restrictions of the United States*. TC Publication 243 (Washington, April 1968), p. 19.

Certainty

The most attractive aspect of quotas is that they can be relied upon to reduce undesired imports to predetermined amounts. Neither demand nor supply, nor even the price, determine the amount of imports. When a tariff duty is introduced or increased, on the other hand, the exact effect cannot be foreseen because reactions of consumers and foreign sellers are uncertain. The domestic producer always risks a change in foreign supply conditions over which he has no control and which can bring an increase of imports despite high duties. Foreign costs may decline, for instance, due to rising foreign productivity, a devaluation of the exporter's currency, foreign subsidies for the industry, or a cost-reducing foreign depression. Even if a tariff is set high enough to leave a margin for such occurrences, the domestic producer does not feel secure. With a quota, on the other hand, he has nothing to fear but a government decision to increase or lift the quota. It is this predictability of imports and the consequent security of the home industry which makes quotas a much stronger protectionist tool than tariffs.

There is, of course, another side to the certainty of import quantities under quotas. It is uncertainty about ensuing changes in costs. By rigidly fixing the supply, the quota places the burden of the market adjustment on prices. In the case of tariffs, on the other hand, the price rise is limited to the rise in the duty, but the price increase in the case of a quota cannot be predicted and may be much greater. Prices in the importing country become quite independent of those abroad and there is no limit to the possible differential developing between world and domestic prices. This disruption of international price ties may cause considerable damage to the economy of the quota country, but it will not of course be regarded as detrimental by those benefiting from reductions made in import quantities.

Discrimination

Tariffs can be used in discriminatory fashion through preferences, or customs unions, or through excessive categorization, but as a rule all trading partners are treated equally under the most-favored-nation clause. Quotas, on the contrary, are basically discriminatory among the countries affected. They are therefore an effective device for rewarding and punishing foreign countries.

Since it is not competition among sellers that determines the source of imports under a regime of quotas, the government of the importing country must select the countries from which to buy and fix the amounts to be bought from each source. The government thus wields great power. It can grant favors for economic and political reasons. It can also obtain concessions for its own exports from trading partners by threatening to reduce or cancel their quotas. Moreover, with direct controls, discrimination can sometimes be practiced without attracting much attention, for even when there is suspicion of discrimination it is next to impossible for a disaffected country to prove its case.

It might be thought that discrimination can be avoided by allocating quotas on the basis of imports in a pre-quota period, and some U.S. quotas are actually distributed today as they were in the 1930s. It is true that this method eliminates some of the aforementioned aspects of discrimination, but the selection of a base period again favors some sources and hurts others. Moreover, performance at some time in history is no justification for a large or small import share ever after. Nor is a historical basis conducive to efficiency: it usually favors old, established interests and traditional sources of supply, while new or improved sources get little or no recognition. This bias may militate especially against the exports of the less developed countries. A recent summary of the findings of six detailed product studies of quantitative import restrictions draws the following conclusions:

> The issuance of import permits is frequently undertaken primarily in favor of "traditional" sources of supply and importers having long-standing relationships with certain foreign producers, limiting market access by newly emerging suppliers in the developing countries. Permissible quota sizes may be unknown or subject to activation under a variety of explicit or implicit trigger mechanisms. The quantity of allowable imports may be highly variable over time, import-calendars may be employed, or "buyers' quotas" may be used under which each allocation is too small to service efficiently. Such administrative techniques frequently appear to result in unfilled quotas as developing-country suppliers, faced with a high degree of uncertainty, are frustrated in their efforts to gain improved and stable market access.

> Even relatively liberal or quasi-automatic licensing of imports on occasion seems to impose a significant burden on developing countries due to complexities involved in securing import permits, attendant costs, delays in issuance, variations in the period of validity, and disclosure requirements as to final purchaser and price.[5]

---

[5] See Ingo Walter, "Nontariff Barriers and the Export Performance of Developing Economies," *American Economic Review*, May 1971, pp. 198, 199.

Although the bias against less developed countries that is inherent in discriminatory policies is a relatively new discovery, it has long been known that this policy instrument is a two-edged weapon in that a country cannot only hurt others in this way but will be hurt by them as well. Trade wars can easily arise when two play this game.

This danger explains the near-unanimous official position against discrimination which has been accepted by most countries and laid down in the rules of GATT. The rejection of discrimination as a legitimate policy tool is also based on long experience: national governments have come to realize that administrative decisions operating without the guidance of freely determined prices lead to misallocation of resources and that the injection of political considerations in the operation of trade results in its shrinkage.

In many instances quotas involve not only discrimination among countries of origin but also among importing and/or exporting firms. The valuable right to import can be assigned in proportion to trade in a fixed base period and so involves the creation of inflexibilities and "not-particularly-deserving vested interests" and the disappearance of efficiency-inducing competitive pressures.[6] In practice trade is frozen into patterns that rapidly become out of date. If, alternatively, quotas are assigned by some arbitrary rules, this granting of monopoly positions involves great dangers of favoritism and even corruption. The problem, of course, is not changed by having an organization of exporters distribute quotas among its members.

Global quotas, permitting all suppliers to import on a first-come first-served basis, are favored by the GATT as nondiscriminatory but are too impractical to be widely used and involve an undesirable method of selection.[7]

The foregoing remarks should be kept in mind in considering the various examples of U.S. quotas discussed in later chapters. These quotas all discriminate by country of origin, while dairy and oil quotas also determine the shares of individual U.S. importing firms.[8] Sugar, meat, textile, and steel quotas, on the other hand, are distributed among firms by the exporting countries' governments or producers' cartels.

---

[6] I owe the term to Leland B. Yeager and David G. Tuerck, *Trade Policy and the Price System* (Scranton, Pennsylvania: International Textbook Co., 1966), p. 49.

[7] Gottfried Haberler, *International Trade* (New York, 1950), p. 348.

[8] The allocation of oil quotas among U.S. importing firms is a good example of the dangers involved in the power of the licensing government. Domestic politics affect the distribution and "inequities become inevitable." William H. Peterson, *The Question of Governmental Oil Import Restrictions* (Washington: American Enterprise Institute, 1959), p. 52.

Profits

The features of quotas discussed so far, flexibility, certainty and discrimination, account for the great effectiveness of quotas as instruments of protection. They are usually listed as "advantages of quotas." But it should be noted that this designation is correct only from the protectionist point of view. Those aspects of quotas, however, to which we now turn, are unfortunate from any point of view. The most important is the profit derived from quotas.

To prevent prices from falling due to foreign competition or to restore prices that are already depressed is the purpose of all import restrictions. This fact is sometimes denied and it is even claimed, with respect to quotas, that the price of a good under a quota is not higher than it would be without it. But it can be shown theoretically and empirically that the price goes up under a quota so long as one assumes that the quota is effective and the price is free. The competition of consumers for a reduced quantity of imported goods must raise their prices and the domestic substitute must be more expensive than the foreign good; otherwise there would be no imports.

When imports are restricted by a tariff, the buyers' added expenditure accrues directly to the importing government's treasury, which hands back these receipts to the public through greater spending or lower taxes. Under a quota, however, the receipts stemming from the price rise go to whoever is lucky enough to have the right to import.

Who will capture this windfall profit depends on the way the quota is administered and on the importers' and exporters' market structure. If the importer is free to select his source of supply among competing exporters, the profit will be his. When quotas are assigned to specific countries, however, the exporters in those countries typically control the allocation of the quota and pocket the profit. This is always true of voluntary quotas, which mean high profits for selected foreign exporters—profits which are, of course, a pure burden on the importer's economy. Thus: "in the case of imported beef, for instance, export prices to the United States from the principal supplier are between 10 and 20 percent higher than the export prices to other countries."[9] But even if all or part of the profit goes to the domestic importer, it represents a redistribution of income that was not intended by those imposing the quota, that is not part of the protectionist purpose, and that involves a loss of welfare.

[9] Council of Economic Advisers, *Annual Report*, 1971, p. 156.

By auctioning off permits to import, the government of the importing country could channel the quota profits into its own coffers. However, such auctioning has hardly ever been used in any country and never in the United States. What the government refuses to do, however, is sometimes done by private beneficiaries. For instance, it was found that "the rights to import a barrel of crude oil (known as 'tickets' in oil industry circles) sell for $1.25, the difference between the domestic and foreign prices."[10]

Quotas are therefore more favorable to profit-receivers than are tariffs. Otherwise, the rise in prices, brought about in either way, will affect the distribution of income according to the class of goods under protection. Its effects can be those of a progressive tax if its heaviest burdens are placed on luxury items. This may be an argument in its favor in less developed countries, but so far as the United States is concerned, there is no doubt that protection is regressive in its income effects because most of the protected goods play a larger role in low-income than in high-income budgets. This is especially true for goods placed under quotas, such as dairy products, meat, sugar, and textiles. Moreover, usually imports of the least expensive items in these classes, like lower quality meat and cheap clothing, are the ones most severely cut by quotas. An additional point is that often the prohibited goods are not produced in the U.S. at all, so that consumers who cannot afford to switch to a more expensive, different type of good have to go without and thus suffer a welfare loss.[11]

Quotas may have monopoly effects. Thus Kindleberger concludes: "A signifiant difference between a tariff and a quota is that the conversion of a tariff into a quota which admits exactly the same volume of imports may convert a potential into an actual monopoly."[12] The decisive point about these effects is that, under quotas, prices can be raised by firms without fear of potential competition from imports. A tariff also reduces import competition and thereby strengthens the market power of domestic industries, but it is much less effective in this respect than a quota.

---

[10] Kreinin, *International Economics*, p. 283.

[11] This point was made with respect to quotas on footwear by Andrew F. Brimmer, Board of Governors of the Federal Reserve System, in an unpublished paper, presented at the Economic Seminar, University of Maryland, November 1970, p. 20.

[12] Charles P. Kindleberger, *International Economics* (Homewood, Illinois: Richard D. Irwin, Inc., 1968), p. 566.

Effect on Exports

Restrictions on the growth of imports tend to inhibit export growth after a while. The effect occurs in a number of ways. One way is for labor and other resources to be pulled away from export industries and into import-replacing industries through price and income adjustments. A more direct route is for foreign countries to reduce their purchases because of a fall in their foreign exchange earnings due to the curtailment of their exports to the import-restricting country. In the case of the less developed countries (LDCs), for example, it has been estimated that a one dollar reduction of imports by the developed countries directly causes a 95¢ fall in the latters' exports to the LDCs.[13]

The most immediate, direct and visible effect of import restriction on exports occurs when imported goods are used as inputs in the production of export goods. This effect is prevented, in the case of duties, by the government's refunding of the extra costs to the exporter. But no such refund is given when costs are raised by quotas on imports. (The probable reason for the absence of such a refund is that the existence of the price differential is not readily admitted and its size not easily ascertained.) Thus the competitiveness of the export goods that require such inputs is reduced.

U.S. exports of petroleum products are especially penalized in this fashion. If the price differential of $1.25 per barrel of crude oil attributable to the import quotas were refunded, this sum would reach up to $354 million for 1967.[14] Nonrefundable cost increases for steel users have similar effects for exporters using steel in the goods sold abroad.

Administrative Costs

There are no estimates of the costs of administering import quotas but it is clear that they are considerably higher than those of administering tariffs. The allocation of quotas and their enforcement require a large administrative apparatus. Government officials have to obtain detailed knowledge on the production and trade of all the varieties of the goods they control. They also have to review the numerous forms that the traders are required to fill out. All this is costly.

---

[13] Bela Balassa, *Trade Liberalization Among Industrial Countries* (New York: McGraw Hill, 1967), p. 195.

[14] Baldwin, *Trade, Growth, and the Balance of Payments*, p. 33.

Furthermore, large costs have to be borne by the trading firms. Their staffs have to devote many hours to detailed plans that have to be made far in advance of sales and cannot easily be adjusted later on. They must keep abreast of changing regulations and fill in almost countless forms. Often they also must pay fees to their trade associations to defray their high costs.[15] All this is a new burden on the economy.

"Voluntary" versus Mandatory Quotas

The term "voluntary" is justified only in the sense that the exporting country has the bitter choice between prohibiting some of its exports or seeing them prohibited by some protectionist measure of the importing country, such as a mandatory quota, a special duty, or even an embargo. The threat of such actions is often reinforced by political pressures.[16]

"Voluntary" quotas were first used by the Japanese in the late 1930s, were rediscovered, with a hefty assist from the United States, in the mid-1950s and quickly became widespread.[17] In the typical cases the Japanese undertook to limit to agreed amounts their exports of specified goods and also to charge no lower than agreed prices. Such agreements are estimated to have covered about 27 percent of the goods exported by Japan to the U.S. in 1963.[18]

The basic features and the economic effects of both types of quotas are generally the same. Both prohibit part of potential imports and allocate the remainder through the importers' government or the exporters' cartels. Both cause the same changes in consumption, production, prices, profits, exports and so on. In deciding the relative merits of the two forms of control, the standards by which they are judged must be kept firmly in mind. This point has to be stressed because the brief comments which make up the literature on voluntary quotas are contradictory. Their lists of the advantages of these quotas include aspects favoring trade liberalization and also aspects favoring trade restriction.

---

[15] John Lynch, *Toward an Orderly Market: An Intensive Study of Japan's Voluntary Quota in Cotton Textile Exports* (Tokyo: Sophia University, 1968), pp. 162, 163.

[16] These threats and pressures are very well and vividly described by John Lynch, ibid., especially pp. 77-94. Cf. also Warren S. Hunsberger, *Japan and the United States in World Trade* (Harper and Row, for the Council on Foreign Relations, 1964), pp. 310-14.

[17] Gardner Patterson, *Discrimination in International Trade: The Policy Issues, 1945-1955* (Princeton: Princeton University Press, 1966), p. 296.

[18] Lynch, *Toward an Orderly Market*, p. 30.

One argument in favor of voluntary quotas from the free-trade point of view is that they are internationally discussed and negotiated before imposition. They thus represent to some extent a compromise between two parties in contrast to unilaterally-imposed mandatory quotas. That the result stems from bilateral negotiations mitigates somewhat the force of exporters' complaints.[19]

Another merit of voluntary quotas is that they can be less rigid than mandatory ones.

> The possibilities of raising quota levels are greater under negotiated export quotas than under the unilateral import quotas. Even though they were not free to act without prior consultation with the United States, and did not dare to propose changes that were too drastic, the Japanese were better off than if any change had required American initiative, probably involving lengthy procedures. Under the "voluntary" system, quota levels were not completely rigid or fixed; the Japanese retained some initiative and used it to enlarge the quotas a little.[20]

On the other hand, most other features of voluntary quotas, which are usually termed "advantages," are in fact highly undesirable from a free-trade point of view. Among these is the expansion in the use of trade restraints brought about by enabling governments to avoid the obstacles which make it difficult to impose mandatory quotas. One such obstacle is the resistance of the public and its representatives to the introduction of mandatory quotas. Few people, in contrast, will be of the opinion that an offer of foreigners to restrain their own exports should be refused. The impression will also prevail that the foreigners' willingness to control their sales indicates that there is something unfair about their competition that justifies intervention.

.The costs of these arrangements to the U.S. economy are also easily overlooked when they are viewed in this fashion. What the public fails to realize is that its interests are likely to be ill-served when agreements are negotiated "behind the scenes and . . . without normal legal processes." In voluntary agreements there are "no Tariff

---

[19] Plenty of bitterness may remain, however, as illustrated by the following quotation from *The Japan Times*, January 18, 1957, p. 6: "Textile manufacturers and exporters . . . accepted the quota figures . . . with unhappiness verging on bitterness. There is no attempt to conceal the feeling that the textile industry here is getting the short end of the deal for political expediency—to preserve friendly trade relations with the United States—and under pressure from the Foreign Ministry." Cited in Hunsberger, *Japan and the United States*, p. 354.

[20] Hunsberger, *Japan and the United States*, p. 355.

Commission investigations, public hearings, or other steps such as would normally permit public discussion. . . ."[21]

Another misconception about voluntary quotas, which tends to make them more acceptable than other measures, is that they are thought to be temporary, emergency devices. In fact they have rarely been lifted and hardly could be.

> Protection will normally induce businessmen to invest too much in an industry and induce too many young people to learn trades there. After a few years it becomes much harder to remove the quotas since to do so would impose serious losses on these individuals. Once we create vested interests, it becomes very difficult to change the policy that supported them.[22]

Far from being temporary, voluntary quotas often prepare the way for mandatory ones. Having gotten used to the former, the public is more ready to accept the latter. Oil and cotton textile quotas in the United States are a case in point. The first voluntary agreement on Japanese textile exports, in 1956, became an intergovernmental agreement after only one year.[23]

Since the arrangements are bilateral, they are also "not subject to established international procedures of review, control, and complaint designed to protect the interest of third countries as well as participants."[24] Policy makers abroad are not fooled by the new and ingenious methods and resent the hypocrisy of exhorting others to obey rules which the U.S. circumvents at convenience.

A serious disadvantage of voluntary quotas when compared to mandatory ones is that the former are likely to be even more discriminatory than the latter. One trading partner may be forced into an agreement while others are left alone. For instance, Japanese exports were restricted while those of its competitors were not. Hence the result of the quota was to replace Japanese exports with exports from Hong Kong, India, Pakistan, and other countries. This discrimination among trading countries is against the basic rules of commercial policy.[25]

---

[21] Ibid., p. 357.

[22] Leonard W. Weiss, *Case Studies in American Industry* (New York: John Wiley & Sons, 1971), p. 191.

[23] Cf. Lynch, *Toward an Orderly Market*, p. 103. See also Baldwin, *Trade, Growth, and the Balance of Payments*, p. 43.

[24] Patterson, *Discrimination in International Trade*, p. 298.

[25] Ibid., p. 299.

A final point is that mandatory quotas may sometimes be assigned to domestic importers while voluntary quotas must, by their nature, be distributed abroad so that the entire quota profit goes to foreign exporters who, therefore, may show little opposition to a system which puts them in a relatively favorable position.

The most important of the obstacles to trade restriction, an obstacle which voluntary arrangements have the "advantage" of overcoming, are the rules of the GATT. These rules, the fruit of great exertions by the United States, were especially devised to prevent such controls.[26] By violating its spirit these measures impair the status of the GATT and undermine respect for international agreements in general.

In sum, the spreading use of "voluntary" quotas tends to offset the progress made in trade liberalization through the lowering of tariffs and the prohibition of mandatory quotas. The old instruments are replaced by an equally powerful new one which so far has escaped all international regulation.

---

[26] For instance, "voluntary" restraints on meat imports to the U.S. are used instead of mandatory quotas, as provided by the Meat Act of 1964, because the latter would violate the GATT.

3

ESTIMATING COSTS

Difficulties of Measurement

In order to estimate the costs of an existing quota it is necessary to compare the actual situation with the hypothetical one that would obtain if the quota were lifted. In most instances not even the data needed to describe the actual situation are readily available, and any estimate of imports, production, and consumption that assumes an existing quota will be abolished has to contend with an almost complete absence of essential information. Therefore, only very few such estimates have been attempted and some authors even consider such attempts hopeless.[1] However, any economic policy is based on judgments of its effects and, if explicit estimates do not exist, recourse must be had to educated guesses. For instance, when a government decides to limit the importation of sugar, it must have some idea, no matter how vague, of the cost of this policy. However unsatisfactory, estimation is necessary.

With some effort it should be possible to collect some useful information bearing on the costs of quotas. The effect on imports, production, and consumption of an assumed abolition of a quota can in fact be roughly estimated in various ways. One can draw upon recent studies of demand and supply elasticities. One can extrapolate pre-quota trends or use trends observed in other countries without quotas. One can also base estimates on the development of non-quota U.S. imports.

Prices represent by far the greatest problem in estimating quota costs. Data on the price of a given good in the importing and in the

---

[1] J. H. Richter, *Agricultural Protection and Trade* (New York and London, 1964), p. 144.

exporting country are rarely available. Prior to the pathbreaking investigation by Kravis and Lipsey no systematic collection of such individual price comparisons existed for the U.S.[2] These authors collected large numbers of price pairs for their study of international competitiveness and found "that it is feasible to collect many types of data relevant to the measurement of international price competitiveness that had never been collected before."[3] Their study is not directed at quotas, however, and it does not cover the goods under quota in the United States.

The present study had to be limited to what little information is readily available. Only for sugar quotas does it offer a complete estimate of different cost components. For textiles there is an estimate of total costs but no breakdown into parts. For oil and meat quotas the estimates of other investigators are presented. In other cases not even crude estimates exist. No total is therefore presented for all the commodities studied here.

Exclusion of Indirect Effects

Direct or "static" costs are those which arise from the quota-induced reallocation of resources exclusive of any change in production *methods*. They include the effects of cuts in imports and consumption and of increases in domestic production and prices. They alone are estimated in this study.

Indirect or "dynamic" costs occur when quotas prevent improvements or cause deterioration in production methods. They arise, for instance, from missed advances of technology and foregone economies of scale in the exporting industries. It is to be expected that these industries would improve their production methods if they were faced with an expanded world market. Their costs and prices thus would become lower than under a quota. The protecting country's industry is also likely to improve its efficiency under the pressure of foreign competition so that the prices of such output as is still home-produced (even without the quota protection) could also be lower than they are under protection. These indirect costs are not estimated here.

The "dynamic" effect, it may be noted, is particularly important when quotas are imposed by a less developed country. Bhagwati terms the loss from "inefficiency in sheltered markets" in countries such as India "gigantic," and remarks: "It is enough to be a consumer

---

[2] Irving B. Kravis and Robert E. Lipsey, *Price Competitiveness in World Trade* (New York: National Bureau of Economic Research, 1971).
[3] Ibid., p. 15.

in India . . . to see the force of this observation!"[4] The loss, though less visible, appears in the U.S. economy also.

Dynamic effects depend greatly on producers' confidence in continued free trade. Fear of an early reintroduction of control would, of course, stifle improvements in production methods. Therefore (though this is rarely considered), the mere threat to impose quotas—such as prevails in the U.S. today—is costly.

Dynamic costs may, in the long run, far exceed static ones. But they can be measured only on the basis of intensive and detailed studies of each of the industries affected by quotas. Such studies are not available, and all one can do is to keep in mind that the static costs covered here are only part of the story.[5]

Types of Direct Costs

The concepts of quota costs of this study are the standard concepts of tariff and quota costs found in the theoretical literature.[6] The widest concept is the "total user cost," which is defined as the reduction in the real income of the users of the controlled good, that is, the amount by which they are worse off than they would be without the trade restriction. Alternatively, one can speak of the benefit that users would obtain if the quota or tariff were removed.

The total user cost consists of *four* components. All four arise from the quota-induced increase in the price of the controlled good to a higher level than would prevail without the quota. This higher price increases the expenditure of users on whatever amount of the good they keep on buying and it also forces some buyers to forego the good.

The four components may be broken down as follows: The *first* part of the buyers' loss represents a gain by the domestic producers of the good. The *second* part is a gain of importers and/or exporters

---

4 Jagdish Bhagwati, "On the Equivalence of Tariffs and Quotas," in Baldwin et al., eds., *Trade, Growth, and the Balance of Payments* (Chicago: Rand McNally and Co., 1965), p. 67.
5 Investigations which demonstrate the dynamic cost-reducing effects of general trade liberalization are discussed in Bela Balassa, *Trade Liberalization Among Industrial Countries* (New York: McGraw-Hill, 1966), pp. 95-97. However, these investigations do not deal with the abolition of specific quotas.
6 This section owes much to the verbalized presentation of the customary geometry in Leland B. Yeager and David G. Tuerck, *Trade Policy and the Price System* (Scranton, Pennsylvania: International Textbook Co., 1966), pp. 45-48. For a recent geometrical presentation, see Ingo Walter, *International Economics* (New York: The Ronald Press Co., 1966), pp. 172-75. For recent refinements of the theory, see W. M. Corden, *The Theory of Protection* (Oxford: Clarendon Press, 1971), pp. 199-201.

of the good. The *third* part pays for the difference between the production cost of the additional domestic output and the costs of the imports that the output displaces. The *fourth* part, finally, is the consumers' loss from switching their purchases to less desirable substitutes.[7]

These four cost elements may be described more fully as follows. The first one, the "transfer cost," arises from the redistributive effect of quotas. The higher price raises the incomes of those domestic producers who would have supplied the good without a quota and at a lower price. Such redistribution is usually the main intended effect of quotas, whether those who impose them look at the effect in this fashion or not. The second component, the "import cost," consists of the expenditure of users of the good on the supply still imported under the quota over and above what they would spend on the same quantity of imports at pre-quota prices. The third component, the "production cost," reflects the production effect of the import limitation on the allocation of domestic productive resources. The cost is brought about by the loss in efficiency connected with the use of resources in producing a good which could be imported more cheaply from abroad. The fourth component, the "consumption cost," consists in the loss of satisfaction suffered by those consumers who, desirous of buying the good at the lower pre-quota price, have to turn to less desirable substitutes because of the higher price caused by the quota.

---

[7] The following notation may be clarifying:

C, I, O: consumption, imports, domestic production under the quota

c, i, o: the differences between C, I, O, and their counterparts without quota.

p: the price differential

$$\text{Then} \quad L_t \text{ (the transfer loss)} = p\left(O - \frac{o}{2}\right)$$

$$L_i \text{ (the import loss)} = p\,I$$

$$L_p \text{ (the production loss)} = p\frac{o}{2}$$

$$L_c \text{ (the consumption loss)} = p\frac{c}{2}$$

$$L_n \text{ (the national loss)} = p\left(I + \frac{i}{2}\right)$$

$$L_u \text{ (the users' loss)} = p\left(I + O + \frac{i - o}{2}\right)$$

$$= p\left(C + \frac{c}{2}\right)$$

The economic significance of the first of these cost items, the transfer cost, differs from that of the others. Since domestic producers are part of the nation, transfer of income from consumers to them does not involve a loss to the nation as a whole. Therefore, this item must be excluded when one is interested in the quota's cost to the nation. The sum of the remaining three items is the "national cost" of the quota, also termed "dead loss" or "dead weight." There is, of course, no point in asking whether the national cost or the user cost is the "better" concept for analysis. Which is to be preferred depends on the question in mind. What is important is to distinguish sharply between the different concepts in evaluating cost estimates.

Cost Concepts Elaborated

Further analysis may help clarify cost measurements. They all have one factor in common: the crucial difference between the actual price of the quota good in the importing country and the potential price, i.e., the price that would prevail if there were no quota. This difference will be termed, for short, "the price differential." It is a key concept in the later chapters.

A closer look at the first item, the money transferred from consumers to producers, reveals two subdivisions. One consists of the extra profit which arises from the price differential that is applied to whatever amount of the good would have been produced at home even if there were no import limitation and no price rise. In cases where a good would not be produced at all in the importing country without quota, this part of transfer cost would, of course, not exist.

The second subdivision of the transfer cost is equal to the profits on the quota-induced additional domestic output. But in this case not all the consumers' extra expenditure caused by the price differential results in producers' profits. Part of the price differential is required to cover the higher unit costs of the additional supply. The fact that this additional supply would not be produced without the price differential proves that its costs must be higher than those of the supply which would come forth also without quota.

To measure transfer costs, one must make an assumption as to the part of the consumers' extra expenditure that goes for producers' profits and the part that goes for higher resource costs. The standard procedure, which is adopted here, is to assign one-half of the expenditure to profits and the other half to resource costs.[8] It follows that the measure of transfer cost on account of additional output is equal to one-half the quantity of such output multiplied by the price differ-

---

[8] Cf. Yeager and Tuerck, *Trade Policy*, p. 46.

ential. To obtain the total transfer cost, this product must be added to the product of the price differential and the quantity produced at home without the quota. As mentioned above, the transfer cost is not a loss to the national economy and hence not a part of the national cost of the quota. Whether the redistribution of income is desirable or not is a separate matter, however, as is brought out later.

The second item, import costs, can under certain circumstances also constitute a mere transfer, in this case from the consumer to the importer. In contrast to the transfer costs described above, however, import costs can also represent a loss to the nation and thus be part of the national cost of quotas. The latter classification is made in the present study for the following reasons.

Import costs are the difference between the receipts of importers or exporters of the amounts of the good admitted under the quota and the receipts that would exist on the same amount of imports at the lower prices prevailing without the quota. Whether this extra income, the quota profit, goes to the exporter or to the importer, or is shared by both, depends on the method of distributing the quota. If the government sells licenses entitling the holder to import the good, the price differential becomes government revenue. If the government merely imposes a global quota or if it licenses domestic importers so that they have an interest in shopping around the world for the lowest priced good, the entire differential, or quota profit, may go to the importers. Under such circumstances the import cost is a transfer cost and not part of the national cost of the quota. But if the importing country allocates the quota by country of origin and leaves the allocation by business firms to the exporting industries, then these industries will act as cartels and the entire quota profit will be theirs. Such is in fact the outcome with all effective voluntary quotas and the same result is also true of some mandatory quotas. The following analysis assumes throughout that this situation is the typical one. Import costs are held to benefit the exporter and are thus part of the national burden imposed by the quota. The import cost is measured by the quantity imported under the quota multiplied by the price differential.

Production costs, the third component of the cost of quotas, arise from the wasteful employment of the nation's resources in the production of goods which could be acquired more cheaply from abroad. Production costs arise only over that range of domestic output which would disappear without the quota. They are by no means the total cost of producing the extra output, but only that part which could be saved by importing the article in question.

The rise in price due to the quota enables producers to expand production because it covers the higher unit costs of the additional output. Some of the additional output incurs costs so high that it would not take place if the price of the good were not raised by the entire price differential. But some advance in output occurs even if the price is only slightly higher than it would be without the quota. The price differential required to call forth the extra output is thus somewhere between the total differential required by the producers with the highest costs and a differential only slightly above zero. It is assumed here, as in the estimation of transfer costs, that the *average* price differential is midway between the extremes. The extra cost of the quota-induced extra output is thus assumed to be split evenly between the extra resource cost and the extra profit connected with this output. The former is the production cost and the latter was included in the transfer cost. Total production cost is thus measured by the quantity of home production provoked by the quota multiplied by half the price differential.

The fourth and last component of the quota cost, the consumption cost, is the sacrifice made by consumers in reducing their consumption of the good below what it would be if there were no quota. The higher price forces buyers to switch from the article under quota, whether imported or home-produced, to less desirable substitutes. For example, instead of buying one dollar worth of foreign cheese kept out by the quota, consumers might buy 80¢ worth of domestic cheese and, say, 20¢ worth of sardines. Since they would have preferred spending their dollar on cheese, they suffer a loss because their wants are less well met than without the quota.

This loss is roughly indicated by the price differential which causes the switch in purchase. Some consumers would continue to buy the good only if its price were the old one. Others stop buying only when the price rises by the entire differential. In between are those who value the difference in satisfaction anywhere along a scale from zero to the full price differential. Therefore, the best approximation of the average value to consumers of the loss per unit of foregone consumption is one-half the price differential. The measure of the consumption cost is then the product of the consumption cut and one-half the price differential.

Combining the three components, import cost, production cost and consumption cost, one finds that the national cost of a quota is measured by the price differential multiplied by the sum of (a) the quantity of imports under the quota, (b) one-half the additional home production, and (c) one-half the cut in the total consumption of the good. The expansion of domestic production plus the consumption cut must equal the import shrinkage caused by the quota. Hence the national cost of a quota can be defined also as the price differential multiplied by the sum of (a) the quota imports and (b) one-half the import shrinkage under the quota.

To obtain the total user cost of the quota, transfer costs must be added to the national cost. It was found above that transfer costs depend on the price differential and on domestic output with and without quota. Adding transfer cost to national cost, one finds that the total user cost is equal to the price differential multiplied by the sum of three items: imports and domestic production under the quota and one-half the difference between the import shrinkage and the domestic output gain due to the quota.

This means that one needs to estimate five items in order to arrive at an estimate of the total user costs of quotas. But since the sum of imports and domestic output under the quota must be equal to consumption under the quota, and since the difference between import shrinkage and output expansion must equal the change in consumption due to the quota, total user cost can also be defined as the price differential multiplied by the sum of consumption under the quota and half the decline in consumption due to the quota.

To illustrate the foregoing analysis: assume that initially 100 units of a good are imported and that this is reduced by a quota to 60 units. Assume further that domestic production was originally 20 units and expands under the quota by an additional 30 units. These 30 units replace part of the 40 units of excluded imports. For the remaining 10 units of former imports, consumers substitute other goods. Assume also that the price of the good is $1 higher with than without the quota.

The total national cost of the quota equals $1 $(60 + \frac{40}{2}) = \$80$.

Of this amount $60 goes to foreign exporters, $15 pays for misallocated resources, and $5 represents loss in consumer satisfaction.

Transfer cost equals $1 $(50 - \frac{30}{2}) = \$35$.

Total user cost equals $80 + $35 = $115.

It might be objected that the foregoing enumeration of quota costs fails to include the cost involved in the decline of exports which will sooner or later follow the import shrinkage. This objection is not valid, however, because exports benefit a country precisely by paying for imports. The loss incurred by switching resources into import substitution is, therefore, also the loss due to switching from the corresponding exports.

4
SUGAR

For many years the production and import of sugar have been subject
to tight and detailed regulation in the United States and other countries. So far as the U.S. is concerned, the present sugar program still
retains the main features of the original Sugar Act of 1934, a typical
piece of restrictive, Great Depression legislation. After suspension
during World War II, this law was restored by the Sugar Act of 1948,
which was amended several times and is still in force today.

Present Arrangements

The Sugar Act contains exact and very detailed provisions regulating
every aspect of sugar production and marketing.[1] Its principal features are the determination of the total sugar supply to be available
to U.S. consumers, the allocation by quota of this total supply to
domestic and foreign suppliers, government payments to domestic
producers, an excise tax on domestic sugar, and a tariff on imports.

The determination of domestic and foreign marketing quotas
proceeds in several steps. First, the act specifies fixed tonnage quotas
for domestic producers (including Hawaii and Puerto Rico), and for
the Philippines, Panama, and Ireland. Second, the Secretary of Agriculture, who is charged with administering the sugar program, determines for each year the total U.S. sugar requirement. Since the
maintenance of a "fair" price for sugar is the law's principal purpose,

---

[1] Cf. U.S. House of Representatives, Committee on Agriculture, *The United States
Sugar Program*, 91st Congress, 2d Session, Washington, 1971, and United States
Tariff Commission, *Quantitative Import Restrictions of the United States*, TC
Publication 243 (Washington, April 1968).

the secretary is required to fix the overall supply at that level which, in his judgment, will result in a price consonant with legislative guidelines. The target price is the average 1957-59 price, adjusted for the changes since that base period in the prices of goods that farmers buy.

Overall supply having been set, it remains to allocate the difference between this supply and the aforementioned fixed home quotas. For this purpose the act provides a schedule specifying each country's percentage share. Setting up this schedule involves the Congress in most difficult and arbitrary decisions as to how large a bonanza to hand each of the numerous applicants and whom to exclude. This painful procedure has to be repeated each time the Sugar Act is extended and the quotas revised. Vague guidelines set up by the Congress for the distribution of sugar quotas are of little use and the consequent wrangling over the handouts is one of the least desirable aspects of the program. Highly paid lobbyists, some former members of Congress, others with close relations to such members, are reported to play a role at times.

The distribution of sugar quotas among foreign countries has become a major problem only with the cessation of sugar imports from Cuba in 1960. Up to that year the bulk of foreign sugar imports was reserved for Cuba (72 percent in 1959) and most of the remainder for the Philippines (22 percent in 1959). There was thus very little to distribute among other countries.[2]

After the break with Cuba, however, its quota became available for distribution among domestic and foreign suppliers. For example, in 1971 the following quotas were assigned: roughly 62 percent of the total requirement was allocated to domestic sources, half of it to domestic beet areas and the other half in about equal parts to (a) mainland cane areas (Florida and Louisiana), and (b) Hawaii, and (c) Puerto Rico. The remaining 38 percent was allocated to 31 foreign countries. The largest foreign quota is held by the Philippines (10 percent of total supply), next comes Mexico, the Dominican Republic, and Brazil with about 5 percent each, then Peru with 3½ percent, Australia with nearly 2, and finally West Indian countries with 1½ percent. Each of the remaining 24 countries' share is less than 1 percent, going down to as little as one-twentieth of 1 percent.[3]

The domestic share of total supply has fluctuated from year to year, but there has been no trend upward or downward. This means that in absolute terms domestic production has increased substantially

---

[2] Based on House Committee on Agriculture, *Sugar Program*, table 8.
[3] Ibid., table 19.

(by about one-third in the last 20 years) since total supply has gone up.

With negligible exceptions, the foreign import quotas apply exclusively to raw sugar. The importation of refined sugar is prohibited except for the Irish quota and small quantities from the Philippines and the Bahamas. Even shipments of refined sugar from U.S. offshore areas (Hawaii and Puerto Rico) are limited. U.S. mainland refineries thus enjoy complete protection. The cost of this protection, for lack of data, is not included in the following analysis of the cost of sugar quotas.

The U.S. government does not fix the price for which imported raw sugar is sold. However, with amounts limited, foreign sellers have no reason to sell for less than the U.S. domestic price. They thus receive this price less the small duty (generally .625¢ per lb.) and transport costs. As is typical of quota regimes, sellers have formed organizations which determine which exporters may sell sugar to the United States. In a number of countries a government monopoly is the sole seller.

Rationale

What is the purpose of this elaborate machinery for the regulation of sugar production? According to the Sugar Act, three major objectives are to be attained: "(1) Make it possible, as a matter of national security, to produce a substantial part of our sugar requirements within the United States by protecting the welfare of those engaged in producing sugar; (2) assure U.S. consumers of a plentiful and stable supply of sugar at reasonable prices; and (3) permit friendly foreign countries to participate equitably in supplying our market for the double purpose of promoting exports of American products and assuring a stable and adequate supply of sugar."

According to its defenders, the sugar program "has been notably successful in attaining all three of these major objectives." It has given us "security of supplies at reasonable cost to the consumer. . . . Retail sugar prices in the United States have been reasonable and remarkably stable since the enactment of the Sugar Act. The act also has been successful in attaining its third objective—the sharing of our sugar market equitably with friendly nations and promoting our export trade." [4]

This rosy picture is open to many serious objections. For instance, in what sense is a price which is 30 to 60 percent above the free market price "reasonable"? The Committee on Agriculture of the House of

---

[4] Ibid., p. 45.

Representatives tries to support its claim by showing that the U.S. price is near the average price in selected sugar importing countries. But what does the price of sugar in Pakistan or Algeria prove about the U.S. sugar price? Nor is there anything remarkable about the stability of a government-controlled price, or about the unusual degree of "assurance and stability of profits." [5]

One may also ask why assurance of a "plentiful" supply of sugar requires elaborate controls while the supply of hundreds of other goods (coffee, tea, rubber, et cetera) takes care of itself. As regards the national security argument, moreover, it seems very hard to imagine a situation where the importation of sugar from Mexico or the West Indies, for example, would present a serious problem.

Terming the present or any other allocation of quotas "equitable" is too devoid of meaning to deserve any comment. But a word may be said about the claim that the sugar program "promotes U.S. exports." [6] The idea seems to be that sugar quotas serve as rewards for countries which import relatively large amounts of goods from the United States. In order to claim that such rewards cause an increase in total U.S. exports one has to show that the presumed rise in exports to rewarded countries exceeds the presumed fall in exports to penalized countries, namely those countries which would sell more sugar to the U.S. without than with quotas. Even in the unlikely case in which such a rise in total exports should occur, it could be brought about through a cash subsidy paid by the sugar consumer to the exporter. Import quotas are an inefficient and costly method of subsidizing exports.

Price Differential

The uncertainty of any benefits from the sugar program contrasts with the certainty of high costs to the nation. The following is an attempt to estimate these costs, however crudely.

World sugar market. As explained in the preceding chapter, one factor needed for such an estimate is the difference between actual U.S. sugar prices and the prices that would prevail in the absence of quotas. An assessment of the latter requires in turn an understanding of the world sugar market. In most major countries sugar production and shipments are under government regulation. Home sugar industries are protected, as a rule, so that about 75 percent of the

---

[5] Ibid., pp. 9, 13.
[6] Ibid., p. 54.

world's sugar is grown in the country where it is consumed. To the extent that imports are permitted, they are frequently subject to preferential arrangements with dependent or formerly dependent overseas countries.

What is called the "world sugar market" is therefore really a market in which only a little less than half—the uncontracted half— of all internationally traded sugar is sold. Moreover, four-fifths of this market is also regulated at present. The International Sugar Agreement of 1968, with a membership of 34 sugar exporting countries, establishes export quotas and aims at supporting sugar prices. Hence the "world price" of sugar is by no means a free market price at present. This price has increased by 65 percent from 1968 to 1970, an increase which undoubtedly is due in large part to the limitations on production imposed by the agreement.[7]

World prices were, in the years without international agreement, more volatile than controlled U.S. prices, but not as volatile as one might infer from pro-quota literature. The median of 11 year-to-year changes, 1959-70, was 6 percent.[8] The movements were rises and falls with no discernible trend over the period under review. The price in 1969 was, for instance, almost equal to the price in 1958 (4.37¢ a pound).

U.S. versus world price. Comparing the behavior of U.S. prices for raw sugar with that of world prices, we find that the year-to-year change in the former, 1959-70, was 3.2 percent. U.S. prices moved almost uninterruptedly upwards, with the price in 1970 (8.07¢) almost 26 percent above that of 1959 (6.24¢). The trend in the U.S. price caused the differential between this price and the world price to increase steadily during the 1960s. From a low of 35 percent in 1960 the differential rose to a high of 61 percent in 1968 (expressed as a percentage of the U.S. price). With the increase in the world price due to the agreement, the differential in 1970 fell back again to 40 percent.

For our purposes it is, of course, not the actual world price that is relevant but the price as it would be if the U.S. abolished its import quotas, reduced its domestic production and bought a larger part of its requirements abroad. How great a rise in world prices would be necessary in the long run in order to bring about an expansion

---

[7] International sugar agreements were in force also in the 1950s.

[8] All price data are from House Committee on Agriculture, *Sugar Program*, table 14, and from U.S. Department of Agriculture, Agricultural Stabilization and Conservation Service, *Sugar Reports*, February 1971, p. 41.

of foreign production equal to the additional U.S. demand? (The larger immediate effect of a sudden switch does not concern us because it is a transition problem to be eased or largely avoided by a gradual changeover.)

Other estimates. Several studies of the costs of sugar quotas have been made but they differ in two important ways from the estimates required for the present study. First, their concern is the world-wide abolition of restrictions, not that of the U.S. alone. Second, they were made before the new international agreement came into force, and thus are based on the low pre-agreement world sugar prices. Both these differences must result in much higher estimates of expected rises in world prices than are appropriate for our study. Nevertheless, the information provided by the existing studies is valuable for the estimates we require.

One of the investigations referred to is by Thomas H. Bates who estimated supply, demand, exports, imports, and prices for 30 sugar producing and/or consuming countries based on 1959 data.[9] According to Bates' estimates, the complete abolition of all sugar quotas would have raised the 1959 world price by about 15 percent. This would have left the world price still about 29 percent below the U.S. controlled price of 1959.

Another estimate of the cost of sugar quotas has been made by R. H. Snape and elaborated upon by H. G. Johnson. Snape's study is based on the years 1959-61 and refers to a "hypothetical world free trade situation" in which all protection and taxation of sugar would be abolished. His conclusion is to regard "5 cents/lb. as being a reasonable free trade equilibrium price for raw sugar, despite the substantial increase in trade that would occur in these circumstances."[10] Johnson's calculations also are based on a world price of 5¢. Compared to the actual world price of 1959-61 this price amounts to an increase by 27 percent due to the freeing of trade.

---

[9] Thomas H. Bates, "The Long-Run Efficiency of the United States Sugar Policy," *American Journal of Agricultural Economics*, October 1968, pp. 521-35. Bates calculated long-run supply functions for 38 sugar suppliers and used the demand functions developed for 55 to 60 countries by A. Viton and F. Pignalosa in "Trends and Forces of World Sugar Consumption," *Commodity Bulletin*, Ser. No. 32, Rome, UN FAO, 1961. Bates also estimated transportation costs. Using a general equilibrium model he obtained estimates of each region's sugar production, exports, imports, and prices. The figures given in the text are derived from Bates' table 6.

[10] R. H. Snape, "Sugar: Costs of Protection and Taxation," *Economica*, February 1969, pp. 35, 36. Harry G. Johnson, *Economic Policies Toward Less Developed Countries* (Washington: The Brookings Institution, 1968), Appendix D, table D-4.

Estimates of present study. If U.S. sugar quotas had been abolished the world sugar price would have been very little, if at all, higher than it actually was in 1970. This is the estimate used in the present study. It is based on the fact that, after the Bates and Snape studies were made, the world sugar price was raised by 65 percent through the International Sugar Agreement. Bates expected a 27 percent rise and Snape and Johnson expected a 15 percent rise from the freeing of the whole world's sugar trade. Their figures would, of course, have been lower had they measured the effect of the abolition by the U.S. alone of sugar protection. With the actual price now 65 percent higher than it was at the time the 15 to 27 percent rises were expected from world free trade in sugar, it seems reasonable to assume that at most a very small further rise would result from U.S. action lifting the quotas.

The same conclusion emerges from the consideration that an import price of 5¢ per lb. for raw sugar, considered necessary by Snape for world free trade in 1959-61, should, if U.S. imports alone were free, be sufficiently high in 1970. (It may be remembered that world sugar prices had no upward trend.) The price of 5¢ per lb. is only 3 percent above the actual 1970 world price of 4.88¢.

The conclusion seems reasonable also in view of the considerable restrictions of supply imposed on producers by the International Sugar Agreement. The expansion of supply without an increase in price is certainly possible. The probable increase in U.S. imports would be roughly from 3.5 million tons to 4.4 million, as will be shown below. This figure amounts to about 15 and 20 percent of present world sugar exports. An expansion of this magnitude should not cause much of an increase in prices under present circumstances. However, to guard against an overestimate of the price differential, we shall calculate the cost of the sugar quotas in 1970 on the assumption of (1) a 3 percent rise in the world sugar price to 5¢ per lb. and (2) an 11 percent rise to 5.5¢.

With the U.S. sugar price in 1970 at 8.07¢ there thus would have been a quota premium of between 2.57¢ and 3.07¢ per lb. In other words, the U.S. price would have fallen by an amount ranging from 32 to 38 percent. This may be compared to the Snape-Johnson assumption of a 33 percent fall in 1959-61 in the U.S. price with complete world free trade, and to the Bates estimate of a 29 percent fall.

In rounded figures price differentials of 2.57¢ and 3.07¢ per lb. amount to differentials of $51 and $61, respectively, per short ton. These figures will be used in the following calculations.[11]

---

[11] Measures in tons are in short tons.

National Cost

Import cost. The import cost, that is, the extra expenditure of users that flows to foreign exporters, is the product of the price differential and the quantity of sugar imported under the quota. Since the latter was 5.2 million tons in 1970, the low estimate of the import cost is $265 million and the high estimate $317 million (see table 1).

Table 1
COST OF U.S. IMPORT QUOTA ON RAW SUGAR, 1970

Line No.	Component of Cost	Symbol	Unit	Estimates	
				Low	High
1	Price differential	p	$	51	61
2	Imports under quota	I	tons, mil.	5.2	5.2
3	Import cost	pI	$ mil.	265	317
4	Half of rise in domestic output	$\dfrac{o}{2}$	tons, mil.	1.55	1.80
5	Production cost	$p\dfrac{o}{2}$	$ mil.	79	110
6	Half of fall in consumption	$\dfrac{c}{2}$	tons, mil.	0.2	0.4
7	Consumption cost	$p\dfrac{c}{2}$	$ mil.	10	25
8	National cost	$p\left(I+\dfrac{o+c}{2}\right)$	$ mil.	354	451
9	Domestic output without quota	O	tons, mil.	2.9	2.4
10	Half of rise in domestic output	$\dfrac{o}{2}$	tons, mil.	1.55	1.80
11	Transfer cost	$p\left(O-\dfrac{o}{2}\right)$	$ mil.	227	256
12	Total user cost	$p\left(I+O+\dfrac{c}{2}\right)$	$ mil.	581	707

Note: See text for explanation of estimates. Line 1: per short ton. Line 8: the sum of lines 3, 5, and 7. Line 9: entry of higher figure under heading "low estimate" is correct. The larger the domestic output without quota, the smaller the quota cost. Line 12: the sum of lines 8 and 11.

Production cost. For an assessment of the production cost an estimate is needed of the amount by which U.S. production would shrink in the absence of quotas. Although this is difficult to calculate, students of the problem seem to agree that about 20 percent to 25 percent of U.S. requirements would still be filled by domestic output.

Very roughly, cane sugar growing would continue, while much of the high cost beet sugar production would close down. Horton "made a rough estimate for internal administrative uses in the early 1960's . . . which indicated that as much as 20-25 percent of our domestic sugar consumption might still come from domestic sources even with [world wide] free trade in sugar." Similarly, Bates predicts a U.S. crop of 20 percent of consumption. Snape's medium estimate, which in his opinion represents the "best guide to the magnitude of the costs involved," implies a domestic production of as much as 32 percent of requirements in the absence of U.S. and foreign quotas.[12]

In this study the low estimate of quota costs assumes that U.S. output without quota would equal 25 percent of consumption and the high estimate assumes home production of 20 percent of consumption. It should be noted that the higher the proportion of home output that is maintained without the quota the lower is the cost of the quota, other things equal. The reason is that a large home output not requiring the quota signifies that relatively few resources are wasted on the larger home production with the quota.

According to estimates given below, U.S. sugar consumption in 1970 would, in the absence of quotas, have amounted to between 11.6 and 12.0 million tons. Home production of 25 percent or 20 percent of consumption thus would amount to 2.9 million tons and 2.4 million tons, respectively. Since U.S. sugar production under the quota in 1970 was approximately 6 million tons, the additional domestic output due to the quota was equal to 3.1 million tons, according to the low estimate, and to 3.6 million tons according to the high estimate. Multiplying half of these tonnages by the price differentials of $51 or $61, one arrives at a low estimate of production costs of $79 million and a high estimate of $110 million (see table 1, line 5).

Consumption cost. Next, one needs to estimate the increase in consumption that would be brought about by a price decline. It appears likely that such an increase would be quite moderate. U.S. per capita

---

12 Donald C. Horton, "Policy Directions for the United States Sugar Program," *American Journal of Agricultural Economics*, May 1970, p. 187; Bates, "Long-run Efficiency," table 6, and Snape, *Costs of Protection and Taxation*, pp. 39, 40.

consumption of sugar has been stable at a high level for many years and the increase which occurred in the last few years did not occur due to falling prices but rather in the face of rising prices.

Estimates of the price elasticity of the demand for sugar in developed countries are, in general, low (around −0.3).[13] The elasticity of U.S. demand for sugar tends to be even lower than that of other countries. The cost estimates of this study use two alternative elasticity assumptions: −0.1 and −0.2.[14] Combined with the low estimate of 32 percent, for the potential price decline without quotas, and a total actual U.S. sugar consumption in 1970 of 11.2 million tons, the low estimate of the foregone consumption comes to around 0.4 million tons. The high estimate, based on a price fall by 38 percent and an elasticity of −0.2, amounts to about 0.8 million tons.

Half of these consumption losses multiplied by the price differential result in consumption costs of $10 million (low estimate) or $25 million (high estimate), as shown in line 7 of table 1. Since the import shrinkage must equal the sum of quota-induced production rise and consumption cut, the estimates imply that imports of between 3.5 million tons and 4.4 million tons were eliminated by the quota in 1970. Imports without quota would have amounted to from 8.7 to 9.6 million tons.

Sum of three cost items. Adding import cost, production cost, and consumption costs, we arrive at the national cost of the U.S. sugar quota in 1970. It amounts to $354 million, according to the low estimate, and to $451 million, according to the high estimate. These figures measure the estimated amounts by which the nation is poorer due to the imposition of sugar quotas.

To put the figures in perspective one may relate them to the total U.S. expenditure on raw sugar in 1970 of $1.8 billion. Hence, the cost of the quota to the nation represented from 20 percent to 25 percent of the total expenditure on this commodity. By far the largest part of

---

[13] Horton, *Policy Directions*, p. 195. The elasticity of world demand implicit in Johnson's calculations (*Economic Policies*) is −0.24, and that implicit in Bates' estimates ("Long-run Efficiency") is as low as −0.14.

[14] The elasticity estimates of the present study take into account the fact that a given percentage reduction in the price of raw sugar means, *cet. par.*, a lesser percentage reduction of the price of refined sugar. A given increase in the quantity bought thus signifies a higher elasticity of demand for refined sugar than for raw sugar. Since consumers respond to the price of refined, rather than to that of raw sugar, we translate assumed elasticities of −0.15 and −0.30 for refined sugar into elasticities of −0.10 and −0.20 for raw sugar. Analysis in terms of refined sugar is prevented by lack of data.

the loss, 70 percent to 75 percent, is import costs, representing un-necessary and easily avoidable subsidies to foreign sugar producers. Those who doubt this point should note that Great Britain, under the Commonwealth Sugar Agreement, pays to its preferred Common-wealth suppliers a price only two-thirds as high as the United States' sugar price.[15] Most of the remaining costs are the production costs that represent the misallocation of U.S. resources. Consumption costs are of minor importance due to the assumption of low demand elasticity.

Transfer Cost

Quotas, in addition to inflicting an economic loss on the nation, also cause a redistribution of income from sugar consumers to producers. Part of the consumers' extra expenditure caused by the price differ-ential goes for sugar that is produced at low cost in the U.S. and would have been produced at home also without price differential. This out-lay therefore pays for an extra profit of low-cost producers. Assuming as before that between 2.9 million tons and 2.4 million tons of sugar would be produced in the U.S. without quotas and assuming again a price differential of $51 or $61 per ton, the income transfer on this account would amount to about $147 million on either basis.

Another part of the extra consumer spending represents extra profits of producers of quota-induced additional output. The cost of this output is higher than the cost of imports would be without quota, but it is not higher by the entire price differential in all instances. We assume that one-half of the extra spending on additional output pays for extra costs, while the other half pays for extra profits. The former is the production cost discussed above, the latter is a transfer payment.

Using the previous estimates of the expansion of U.S. sugar pro-duction caused by the quota (3.1 million tons or 3.6 million tons), we find that the transfer cost on this second account amounts to between $79 and $110 million. Thus the total transfer cost caused by sugar quotas in 1970 comes to between $227 million and $256 million (table 1, line 11).

Total User Costs

Adding the transfer cost to the national cost of the sugar quota, one finds that the total users' loss would have amounted in 1970 to $581

---

[15] *The Economist*, May 22, 1971, p. 66.

million, according to the low estimate, and to $707 million, according to the high estimate. These figures represent from 32 percent to 39 percent of the total expenditure on raw sugar.

The foregoing estimates cover only the costs of raw sugar quotas. The additional cost of the almost complete protection of sugar refining is not included for lack of data. International trade in refined sugar is so small and so tightly controlled that a meaningful world price of refining cannot be ascertained. What such a price would be without protection is even more uncertain.

There is little doubt, however, that refining margins, at least on the U.S. mainland, "are in general significantly higher than those on the world market."[16] Yet the prohibition of imports of refined sugar from foreign and even U.S. offshore refineries appears to be justifiable to the House Committee on Agriculture on the grounds that "unrestricted imports of refined sugar would seriously reduce the volume of mainland refining and would create price problems."[17] It is thus safe to assume that substantial additional savings could be had if the lower costs of foreign and of U.S. offshore refineries could be utilized.

Final Observation

It might be argued that a part of the loss suffered by the U.S. because of the sugar quotas should be viewed as a form of aid extended to poor countries. But there is little truth in this argument. After all, the allocation of the quotas among countries can hardly be explained by their relative needs. Why should a rich country like Australia, for instance, receive a gift of about $13 million in 1970, or South Africa nearly $4 million, not to mention Ireland's little bonanza of $300,000 (for a sugar importing country, to boot).[18] Moreover, because the aid depends on sugar production it induces some countries to produce a good for which they are not particularly well suited while leaving other countries, suited for such production, a long way from capacity output.

---

[16] Snape, *Costs of Protection and Taxation*, pp. 34, 36. Snape assumes world refining costs of between 1.25 and 1.75¢ per lb. with world free trade in refined sugar, 1959-61. His estimate of the world loss from quotas on refined sugar, 1959-61, is more than 60 percent higher than his estimate of the loss from raw sugar quotas (p. 40). For 1970 this estimate appears too high, however.

[17] House Committee on Agriculture, *Sugar Program*, p. 13.

[18] In this context the relevant price differential is between the U.S. price and the actual world price in 1970, as distinct from the potential world price used in the loss calculation.

The arbitrary method of distributing quotas among countries also makes lobbying almost unavoidable. For with each extra thousand tons bought by the U.S. worth about $64,000, lobbyists are likely to be well paid by those seeking larger quotas. Part of the income stemming from quotas is thus probably dissipated in payments to lobbyists. Also, some of this income goes not to foreign producers but to American firms which acquire land abroad in the expectation of obtaining a sugar quota making their investment profitable.

For political reasons the sugar program is not likely to be abolished in the near future. Modification of the program is possible, however, and should be guided in the right direction by awareness of the program's implications. A number of well conceived, practical proposals for the revision of the Sugar Act have in fact been made in recent years by, among others, Representative Findley and Professor Horton.[19]

One proposal is to stop further expansion of high-cost U.S. sugar production. To curb additional output, of course, does not involve the hardships connected with abandoning or reducing existing operations. U.S. production has increased by about one million tons or about 20 percent during the 1960s. Surely, this growth need not continue. A slight reduction of the target price of sugar and the reduction or elimination of direct payments could achieve this modest goal.

The second proposed reform is to channel to the Treasury all or part of the $265 to $317 million now distributed as quota premium to foreign exporters. This change can be carried out by charging an import fee, such as the one provided in the 1962 legislation but allowed to expire in 1964. Since then several drafts of sugar bills reintroduced such a fee but they were always dropped in the final legislation. If one started with a small fee and then gradually increased it, one could effect a smooth transition to the total elimination of foreign quota profits.

A more radical reform, which however still would leave the U.S. industry untouched, would be to sell the rights to import to the highest bidders. In addition to earning income for the Treasury, this measure would have the great merit of directing sugar production to those countries most suited for this industry; in other words, it would be a move toward efficiency. It would also help eliminate lobbyists, who in protection of their benefits oppose all reform in the existing system.

---

[19] Horton, *Policy Directions*, pp. 190-95. Speech by Representative Findley, *Congressional Record*, January 21, 1971, p. H18.

5
TEXTILES

Introduction

Of all the quotas in force in the U.S. today, those covering textiles are among the most costly.[1] Very roughly, the burden imposed on U.S. consumers by textile quotas is of the same order of magnitude as the cost of oil quotas. Moreover, textile quotas not only are damaging to the U.S. economy, but also are especially damaging to the economies of less developed countries because they slow down the growth of their most promising export industry, an industry which—in contrast to oil production—is not limited to countries with special resource endowment.

Defenders of quotas claim, of course, that prohibiting imports does not raise prices and thus does not impose any cost on the U.S. economy. But since they tell us in the same breath that the American industry cannot possibly compete with a "flood" of cheap imports, we need not take this claim seriously. If any evidence were needed, one could point to the fact that a share in the quota can be bought for a price, a price which, naturally, is paid in the last resort by the consumer.[2]

Despite quotas and high tariff barriers, the textile industry has been calling for additional protection these last 35 years.[3] What are

---

[1] The textile industry comprises the output of textile mill products and of apparel and related products.

[2] "Cotton quotas are bought and sold by one manufacturer from another. For example, if a manufacturer has a large order and an insufficient quota, he simply 'buys' the quota from another manufacturer. Obviously, his price is increased." U.S. Congress, Committee on Ways and Means, *Hearings on Tariff and Trade Proposals*, 91st Congress, May 21, 1970, p. 1554 (hereafter cited as *Hearings*).

[3] There is "a general tendency of U.S. tariffs to bear more heavily on labor-intensive manufactures than on other goods." Hal B. Lary, *Imports of Manufactures from Less Developed Countries* (New York: National Bureau of Economic Research, 1968), p. 129.

the reasons for its complaints? Is the industry in a process of contraction and are quotas requested to slow down a painful transition? Such is the impression received from the pro-quota literature, but the fact is that the volume of textile production in the U.S. has grown by 43 percent from 1960 to 1970 and is still growing (table 2). The issue thus is not of preventing the demise of an industry, but rather of stopping its further growth and starting it toward gradual contraction. The distinction should not be lost sight of throughout this discussion.

Labor-Intensive Industry

The textile industry uses relatively more labor and less capital than most other industries and is therefore less suited than almost any other industry to an advanced industrial economy and more suited to countries rich in labor and poor in capital. It will be objected that this is no longer true, the industry today being highly mechanized and capital-intensive. But this view overlooks the fact that *all* industries have moved in this direction and that it is the relative position of an industry that matters.

The question has been thoroughly analyzed by Hal B. Lary who concludes that textiles still rank among the most labor-intensive industries.[4] He refutes a 1965 report prepared by the Special Committee on Textiles of the Organization for Economic Cooperation and Development (OECD) and published under the title *Modern Cotton Industry—A Capital-Intensive Industry*. "Only a few years ago," the committee states,

> it was usual for the textile industry to be cited by economists as one of the so-called "labour-intensive" industries, i.e., those whose production depends primarily on manpower. Although this may still be true for certain branches of the textile industry, it is no longer so for cotton which is increasingly becoming a capital-intensive industry with investments easily amounting to $20,000 per work-place.

This transformation, the report goes on to say, is "practically complete in the United States and Japan, but still slowly proceeding in Europe."

Lary shows that the OECD assertion is not borne out by the facts. He uses his ingenious measure of labor intensity: the industry's value added per employee (roughly, value of output minus value of materials used divided by employment). By this criterion the higher the

---

[4] Ibid., pp. 80-85, chart 1, and table 2.

value added per employee, the more capital-intensive the industry, and the lower the value added per employee, the more labor-intensive it is. "This measure may be taken to reflect the flows of services into the manufacturing process from both human capital and physical capital, and permits their treatment on a common basis."[5]

In the apparel industry, the value added per employee was only 49 percent of the U.S. national average in 1965. This figure was the lowest of all major industries and also the lowest of all 102 major and minor industries listed by Lary. In textile mills products, value added per employee was 64 percent of the national average. A lower figure is found only for the following industry groups: lumber and wood, rubber footwear, leather and leather goods, boatbuilding and repairs, and watchcases.

Lary concludes:

> In brief, the evidence considered for the United States is consistent with the view that there has been heavy investment in modernization in the last few years in cotton textiles, but it gives little reason to think that the industry is becoming capital-intensive compared with manufacturing in general and ceasing to be appropriate to the factor endowments of the less developed countries. According to the criteria applied in this study, cotton textiles and the textile industry in general still rank among the most labor-intensive of the manufacturing industries. . . .
>
> The contrary view that a fundamental change in textiles is under way may rely unduly on comparisons with the industry's own past characteristics and performance, and fail to allow for the progress made by manufacturing in general. The illustrations frequently given of developments in the industry also suggest a tendency to confuse the technological optimum with average practice at any one time.[6]

The widely held view that textiles are one of the best, if not the best, manufacturing industry for LDCs rests on such findings.[7]

The industry's spokesmen, far from denying its labor intensity, regard it as a principal merit. At congressional hearings the greatest emphasis is regularly placed not only on the number of jobs at stake, but also on low skill requirements.

---

[5] Ibid., p. 14.

[6] Ibid., pp. 84-85.

[7] See, e.g., Gardner Patterson, *Discrimination in International Trade: The Policy Issues* (Princeton: Princeton University Press, 1966), p. 321.

Textiles is a business which relies heavily on semiskilled workers, workers who do not have the type of occupational dexterity and mobility that others may have. . . . We do have in this country a need for certain types of production, which are made up largely of high labor costs—that is a high percent of the total cost is in labor—just as do other countries of the world, whether they be developed or undeveloped countries.[8]

If this reasoning were valid, one would have to reproach the textile industry for having mechanized at all. Surely, more unskilled jobs could be provided if there were no sewing machines, for instance. By the same token, one also could argue (as some have) that bulldozers should be prohibited because pick-and-shovel road building requires large numbers of unskilled workers. In Keynes' classic words: "If protectionists merely mean that under their system men will have to sweat and labour more, I grant their case. . . . The protectionist has to prove not merely that he has made work, but that he has increased the national income. . . . Is there anything that a tariff could do, which an earthquake could not do better?"[9]

To preserve the status quo means to continue to attract new generations of workers into relatively low-paying occupations at a high cost to consumers in this country rather than to spend money to upgrade these workers' skills and to transfer them into other occupations. The mobility of resources is all-important in the face of advancing technology. How quickly the status quo is becoming obsolete can be seen from the fact that Japan is already regarding parts of the textile industry as unsuitable for a country of its stage of development. It is, for instance, building factories in Taiwan to knit sweaters for sale in Japan.

Cotton Textile Quotas

As for many restrictive policies, textile quotas were first introduced in the 1930s. At that time a great tidal wave of Japanese cotton goods came into the United States. An increase in the tariff on cotton goods by 42 percent had little effect and the industry pressed for quotas. The U.S. government, however, was opposed to an official introduction of quotas because it conflicted with its principles of commercial policy. In this situation the then president of the Cotton Textile Institute in New York, Dr. Murchison, had the novel and

---

[8] *Hearings*, May 20 and 21, 1970, p. 1214, statement by John C. West, lieutenant governor, South Carolina, and p. 1424, remark by Chairman Wilbur D. Mills.
[9] John M. Keynes, *The Nation and Athenaeum*, December 1, 1923.

brilliant idea of concluding a purely private agreement between the Japanese and the U.S. textile industries. By this agreement, which was in effect from 1937 to 1940, the Japanese industry, represented by the Japan Cotton Spinners' Association, put quota limitations on itself.[10]

When imports of cotton textiles from Japan again increased rapidly in the mid 1950s, the U.S. cotton industry became upset again and feared disruption of its market. Various means of protection were tried, such as boycotts of imported goods, discriminatory state laws, and escape clause actions, but such measures brought little relief. The 1937 agreement, however, lived in the memory of American textile people.

An arrangement between the two industries like the one of 1937 was not feasible any more since the anti-trust laws had in the meantime "evolved to a point where it is now regarded as impermissible for direct discussion on the subject of trade restrictions to take place between Japanese and American cotton manufacturers."[11] But the same effect could be attained by a unilateral undertaking of the exporters to put quotas on their shipments to the U.S.

The first public suggestion of a "voluntary" quota was made in the U.S., according to Lynch, by J. Craig Smith, then president of the American Cotton Manufacturers' Institute, in April 1955. From then on pressure for cotton textile quotas continued in the U.S., causing the Japanese government to fear that protectionist measures would be taken. To prevent them, in December 1955, the Japanese Ministry of Trade and Industry announced the new policy of quotas, effective January 1, 1956. (Thus, the last year of uncontrolled cotton imports was 1955.) The most important points of the ministry's statement were: "The volume of cotton fabrics to the U.S. for 1956 will be restricted to 150 million square yards. . . . For certain items which are especially liable to compete with American products, export volumes will be adjusted item by item. . . . Export prices will be strictly maintained to prevent charges of under pricing."[12]

[10] John Lynch, *Toward an Orderly Market: An Intensive Study of Japan's Voluntary Quota in Cotton Textile Exports* (Tokyo: Sophia University, 1968), pp. 91-97. This chapter owes a great deal to Lynch's excellent study. Information was also obtained from Robert C. Sherman, Department of Agriculture, unpublished talk at the Agricultural Outlook Conference, November 1961, Washington, D. C., on "The Complex Problem of Cotton Textile Imports," pp. 6-11.

[11] Warren S. Hunsberger, *Japan and the United States in World Trade* (New York: Harper and Row, published for the Council on Foreign Relations, 1964), p. 317.

[12] Lynch, *Toward an Orderly Market*, p. 102. See also Patterson, *Discrimination in International Trade*, p. 297.

Because the U.S. industry was not satisfied and continued to press the government for action, the private agreement was replaced, after only one year, by an "official" agreement, approved by the U.S. government. This accord covered all categories of cotton textile imports and reduced the 1956 ceiling from 150 million yards to 113 million.[13] The U.S. textile industry, however, was not much helped by this 1957 agreement because other countries' exports replaced the excluded Japanese ones. Imports from such other countries rose from $3.6 million in 1956 to $108 million in 1960. The most important of these newer suppliers were Hong Kong, India, Portugal, Spain, Egypt, Taiwan, Korea, Okinawa, Pakistan, and Israel.[14]

The fact that the export restrictions negotiated with Japan were nullified by increased imports from other sources led the U.S. government to new and much more far-reaching protectionist steps that affected all nations exporting or importing cotton textiles. In 1961 the U.S. requested the GATT to call a conference of textile importing and exporting nations to work out some solution to the problems of textile trade. At this conference a short-term (one-year) cotton textile agreement was negotiated, to be followed a few months later by a long-term accord (October 1962). This long-term agreement (LTA) regarding international trade in cotton textiles ran initially for five years and was extended for three years in 1967 and again in 1970.

The agreement authorizes all participating importing countries, despite the general GATT rule against quotas, "to limit imports of specified cotton textile goods which it found were disrupting or threatening to disrupt its markets." The importing country can request the exporting country to limit its shipments. If the exporter does not accede to this demand, the importer may "decline to accept imports above the level of the preceding year." Faced with such a "choice" most exporting countries preferred concluding agreements with importing countries, specifying "voluntary" limits on the quantity of the various items to be sold. The U.S. has such agreements with 27 exporting countries, accounting for 90 percent of U.S. imports of cotton textiles.[15]

Needless to say, to the importing countries "adjustment" of the cotton textile industry, as contemplated in the LTA, did not mean

---

[13] Lynch, *Toward an Orderly Market*, p. 109.

[14] Sherman, "Cotton Textile Imports," p. 7.

[15] U.S. Tariff Commission, *Quantitative Import Restrictions of the United States*, TC Publication 243 (Washington, D. C., April 1968), pp. 60, 61. Also, Stanley Nehmer, "Remarks Prepared for Delivery to the American Management Association's Manufacturing Conference," New York City, March 17, 1971 (unpublished), p. 11.

transferring resources out of cotton textile production. On the contrary, it meant increasing the efficiency of the industry, largely through making it more capital-intensive.[16]

Non-Cotton Quotas

The Japanese have also imposed export controls on woolen and man-made textiles in the 1960s. An official list of the items affected is not available but, for 1965, Lynch mentions woolen fabrics, gloves, sweaters, rayon products, and silk fabrics. These "voluntary" quotas are administered similarly, as in the case of cotton textiles, by the Ministry of Trade and Industry and the trade associations.[17]

In recent years these controls have not prevented a very rapid rise in the U.S. import of man-made textiles, which are even outstripping cotton goods in importance. Therefore, in 1969, the U.S. government tried to arrange an international agreement similar to the LTA to cover wool and man-mades. This agreement would have required countries not participating to be enjoined from taking unfair advantage of those accepting the agreement. But it was refused by other countries and GATT itself.

Thereupon the U.S. proposed to Japan, in the same year, a comprehensive bilateral agreement covering all wool and man-made fiber textile products. This proposal and similar ones made in the following months were also rejected.[18] In 1971, however, the U.S. government set a deadline for Japan either to limit its exports of wool and man-made textiles to the U.S. in a fashion acceptable to American industry or be faced with legislated quotas regardless of their illegality under GATT rules. Despite the resistance of the Japanese industry, the Japanese government submitted to U.S. demands, partly for political reasons, and signed a "memorandum of understanding" along the lines indicated.

The agreement limits the overall growth of exports of man-made textiles from Japan to the U.S. to 5 percent a year and that of wool products to 1 percent a year for the next three years. The base period is the year ending March 1971. The most important features of the agreement are the specific limits already set on 18 categories of goods and to be set in the future on any additional items as soon as they threaten American products. It is these quotas on individual items

---

[16] Patterson, *Discrimination in International Trade*, pp. 311, 316, 317.

[17] Lynch, *Toward an Orderly Market*, p. 199 and Appendix II.

[18] Maurice H. Stans, "Statement before the House Ways and Means Committee on H.R. 16290," May 12, 1970, pp. 8, 9.

which American producers were most anxious to obtain because they imply ironclad protection. The permitted growth rate for some specific items is as low as 2½ percent per year.

The other main exporting countries, Taiwan, Korea and Hong Kong, have signed similar agreements. These countries are allowed a growth rate of 7 to 7½ percent instead of the 5 percent prevailing for Japan.[19]

Administration

Administration of import quotas is always difficult and costly, but never so much as for textile quotas, which require an enormous variety of ever-changing products to be classified and decided upon. The principles and procedures followed can have as much influence on the industry as the size of the quota allotted to it. For example, under the present long-term agreement on cotton a newly exporting country will not begin by testing the market but will try to start out directly with large shipments in order to establish a high "historical basis." A committee of six high U.S. government officials, each representing a different department, will then convene and make difficult decisions as, for example, how many cotton gloves of a certain type may be imported from Haiti. When the newcomer's sales have increased to a certain point, a "voluntary" bilateral agreement will be negotiated and future imports will be subject to this agreement.

The execution of such an agreement may be controlled on the United States side, as is done for imports from Korea and Taiwan, for instance, or an export control system may be used where such a system is found reliable and preferred by the exporting country, as, for instance, Japan and Hong Kong. The distribution of quotas among exporting firms is always handled in the exporting country. In the case of Japan the quota program is administered jointly by the Japanese government and cotton textile trade associations. But a very large portion of the work, including the allocation of most of the quotas, is in the hands of the big export associations.

A firm's quota is determined partly by the quantity of its exports in a base period and partly by the price at which it sells. The purpose of paying attention to price is to penalize firms charging too low a price. Balance-of-payments considerations are among the reasons for striving to prevent low prices.

---

[19] *The New York Times*, October 16, 1971, p. 10, and Department of Commerce, Office of Textiles, unpublished tables.

When a Japanese firm with an unfilled quota wishes to fill an American order it must apply through the Exporters' Association to the Ministry of Trade and Industry. The ministry has the power to reject such an application for an export license despite the firm's unfilled quota. Among the reasons for rejection is that the contract price may be too low in the view of the government official.

The system most certainly increases the selling costs of the products falling under the quotas. The preparation of plans long before the commencement of the selling year requires much more time and effort than is ordinarily given to sales planning by trading companies. Because of the danger of penalties, especially the partial loss of a quota allocation, the planners realize they are doing more than setting targets. The breakdown into quarters, while helping orderly marketing, can involve a serious miscalculation that must be lived with. It can be most distressing to discover late in the year, when there is a shortfall in sales in the final quarters, that somewhat more than the planned quantities could have been sold in the early quarters. This planning involves the patent cost of more than the normal amount of man-hours devoted to it, and the occult costs (opportunity costs) involved in not using the same human talent for the company's basic work of opening up new markets and improving old ones.

Other costs include the fees paid the associations for each square yard exported. The individual fees are small in themselves—although they are on low-priced goods for the most part—however, their sum becomes quite substantial when multiplied by millions. These fees go toward the payment of the high cost of administering the controls. Thus, they are a necessary consequence of the quotas themselves.[20]

Trends in Production and Trade

From small beginnings textile imports rose rapidly in the 1960s. Their volume tripled and their dollar value was three-and-a-half times as great in 1970 as in 1960. The rise accelerated in the second half of the decade when imports about doubled, whether measured by volume or by value, as compared to a rise by two-thirds in the first half of the decade (tables 2 and 3).

That such high growth rates should impress observers and cause concern among domestic producers is to be expected. But when

---

[20] Lynch, *Toward an Orderly Market*, pp. 162, 163.

Table 2

TRENDS IN U.S. TEXTILE CONSUMPTION, IMPORTS AND IMPORT-CONSUMPTION RATIO, 1960-70
(millions of pounds)

	1960	1965	1970	(Index 1960 = 100) 1965	1970
Domestic Production					
Cotton	4,198	4,477	3,815	107	91
Wool	333	371	253	111	76
Man-made	1,852	3,362	5,083	182	274
Total	6,383	8,210	9,151	129	143
Consumption					
Cotton	4,217	4,664	4,088	111	97
Wool	393	461	345	117	88
Man-made	1,880	3,456	5,532	184	294
Total	6,490	8,581	9,965	132	154
Imports					
Cotton	252	361	472	143	187
Wool	63	96	96	152	152
Man-made	28	93	455	332	1,625
Total	343	550	1,023	160	298
Ratio of Imports to Consumption	%	%	%		
Cotton	6.0	7.7	11.6		
Wool	16.0	20.8	27.9		
Man-made	1.5	2.7	8.2		
Total	5.3	6.4	10.3		

Note: Consumption equals domestic production plus imports minus exports. Exports are not shown in this table.

Source: Cotton and Wool, 1960: U.S. Department of Commerce, Office of Textiles, Trade Analysis Division, *Cotton, Wool and Man-made Fiber Textiles, Tables Depicting United States Foreign Trade* (unpublished), March 1971.

Man-made fiber textiles, 1960: Textile Economics Bureau, *Textile Organon*, February 1971.

1965 and 1970: Office of Textiles, *Cotton, Wool, and Man-made Fibers Manufactures,* March 1971.

growth starts from a very low level, high percentage rates give an exaggerated impression. This applies particularly to the spectacular rise in the imports of man-made textiles which started from next to nothing and amounted to very little until 1966. Yet man-made textiles accounted for more than three-quarters of the textile import

Table 3

TRENDS IN U.S. TEXTILE IMPORTS, 1960-70

(millions of dollars)

	1960	1965	1970	(Index 1960 = 100) 1965	(Index 1960 = 100) 1970
Cotton	269	369	536	137	200
Wool	216	357	358	165	166
Man-made	61	193	1,049	316	1,720
Total	546	919	1,943	168	355

Source: U.S. Department of Commerce, Office of Textiles, Trade Analysis Division, *Cotton, Wool and Man-made Fiber Textiles, Tables Depicting United States Foreign Trade* (unpublished), March 1971.

growth from 1965 to 1970. Wool imports stopped growing after 1965 and cotton imports after 1966. The latter had represented the bulk of textile imports at the beginning of the decade, but their share in the total fell between 1960 and 1970 from 73 percent to 46 percent in volume and from 49 percent to 28 percent in value.

The growth of imports does not signify by any means that the U.S. textile industry was shrinking in the 1960s. On the contrary, its output expanded by 43 percent in that period. The figures in table 2 give the impression of a considerable slowdown in this growth during the second half of the decade, but this is largely due to the recession-induced decline of 1970. Thus, the production index for 1969 was 151 and the rise during the four years 1965 to 1969 was 17 percent.

There has been a sharp shift within the industry, away from cotton and wool into man-made fibers. But the decline in cotton and wool production in 1970, shown in table 2, is again partly due to the recession.

Viewing the industry as a whole, however, there has been no retrenchment as yet. Resources have not moved away from, but rather have moved into, this industry despite the comparative disadvantage of many of its parts as against less industrialized countries.

Since imports and exports were small, the foregoing remarks about textile production hold in general also for textile consumption, which is the sum of home production and imports minus exports. Consumption of all textiles grew by more than 50 percent during the 1960s, while that of man-mades tripled.

What matters most for this study are the changes in the ratio of imports to consumption. Lacking the data for comparing the dollar value of imports to that of consumption, the best one can do is to measure the relation in terms of quantities. However, it should be noted that ratios based on quantities are higher than ratios based on dollar values since prices of imported goods are, on the average, lower than those of domestic goods. Consequently, quantity ratios overstate the economic significance of imports.

The share of imports in U.S. textile consumption was a negligible 5 percent in 1960 and, having doubled during the decade, was still only 10 percent in 1970. In view of the strong pressure for quotas in that year, it is particularly noteworthy that only 8 percent of man-made textiles came from abroad in 1970. According to preliminary estimates, this ratio may have risen to around 11 percent in 1971, a rise to which the imminence of import controls may have contributed.

The low ratios indicate that imports play an insignificant role in large areas of the industry. Examples are the production of yarns and fabrics, and hosiery and underwear. But low overall ratios are compatible with very high ratios for selected products. Outstanding examples are sweaters, 72 percent of which were imported in 1969, men's woven shirts with 38 percent, women's slacks and shorts with 33 percent, and so on.[21] Clearly a small firm specializing in one of these affected articles is not helped by the fact that overall ratios are low. But it is equally clear that in such instances of foreign superiority the domestic producer should be assisted in leaving the industry rather than frozen into it by prohibiting the importation of the cheaper foreign product.

Cost Estimates

The difficulties encountered in estimating the cost of sugar quotas are child's play compared to those one faces with regard to textile quotas. In part this is due to the size of the textile industry and the enormous variety of its products. But the problem is due also to a lack of relevant data, despite the great mass of textile statistics.[22] In fact,

---

[21] U.S. Tariff Commission and American Apparel Manufacturers Association, quoted in *Hearings*, May 20 and 21, 1970, p. 1385. Note that dollar ratios are only a fraction of quantity ratios in some instances.

[22] Lary has done a great deal of work matching U.S. production of textiles and textile imports (*Imports of Manufactures*, table C-1). Ratios of imports to domestic production by type of product have also been prepared by the Bureau of the Census in *U.S. Commodity Exports and Imports as Related to Output, 1965 and 1966* (Washington, D. C., 1968). But apart from the fact that these comparisons have not been updated, they do not provide the information needed for quota cost estimates.

only a single study of the quota costs seems to have been made to date.[23]

The best that can be done within the scope of this study is to give a rough idea of the magnitude of the subsidy provided by American consumers to the textile industry. The estimate will be confined to the total user cost of textile quotas. A breakdown into the categories of costs discussed earlier cannot be attempted in this case because of data shortages.

Before plunging into the problems of estimation, the main results can be stated here: the total cost of textile quotas in future years will be the sum of the cost of quotas on cotton goods, in force for many years, and the cost of import quotas imposed in October 1971 on woolen and man-made textiles.

Consumer expenditures on cotton textiles were, already in 1970, probably at least $600 million higher than they would have been without quotas. The newly-imposed quotas on woolen and man-made textiles may add about $1,900 million to consumers' costs in 1972. The total cost of textile quotas in 1972 is thus estimated tentatively at $2,500 million. In a few more years, as the gap between permitted and potential imports widens, the loss will mount. By 1976 it may easily reach $1,100 million on cotton goods and $3,600 million on wool and man-made goods. (Hereafter the sum of woolen and man-made textiles will be designated as non-cotton textiles, although it excludes other non-cotton goods such as silk.)

The foregoing estimates are, of course, highly tentative and should be interpreted only as rough indications of the probable magnitudes. The following description of the derivation of the figures should enable the reader to use his own judgment and to make whatever adjustments he deems appropriate.

Consumption. To avoid confusion it should be noted, first, that the cost calculations for textiles rely entirely on dollar value data in contrast to the estimates for sugar which utilized price and quantity data. Even in value terms the first piece of information required is lacking: the total U.S. expenditure on finished textile goods. It is approximated by adding the sum of two items of personal consumption expenditure: "clothing and accessories except footwear" and "semidurable house furnishings." In 1970 the former was $44,300

---

[23] This study, "Import Controls and Domestic Inflation" by Federal Reserve Board Governor Andrew F. Brimmer (November 1970, mimeographed), is discussed in the technical note to this chapter.

million and the latter $6,400 million. This gives a total U.S. consumer expenditure on textiles of $50,700 million in 1970.[24]

Next, the shares of cotton and non-cotton goods in total textile consumption must be estimated in order to distinguish between the cost of the old cotton quotas and the new non-cotton quotas. For want of value data these shares must be approximated with the help of quantity data. In terms of pounds the share of cotton in total consumption was 40 percent in 1970. In terms of dollars the share must be lower, however, since the price of cotton is lower than that of non-cottons.

In textile imports, where the shares of each fiber are known in both value and volume terms, the figures for 1970 are 28 percent for the former and 46 percent for the latter. The corresponding adjustment of cotton's share in consumption from quantity to value terms yields the result that the expenditure on cotton textiles amounted to 24 percent of the expenditure on all textiles in 1970. The total $50,700 million expenditure on textiles is thus deemed to consist of a $12,200 million expenditure on cotton textiles and a $38,500 million expenditure on woolen and man-made textiles.[25]

Price differential. As already noted, the crucial factor in quota costs, and also the most difficult one to estimate, is the price differential, the difference between the price of goods with and without quotas. For cotton textiles, with-quota prices are the current prices in the U.S., while the without-quota prices could be inferred from prices prevailing in the countries of origin and in such importing countries as do not impose quotas. However, the work involved in collecting such comparable prices has not been undertaken to date, as far as I know.

For woolen and man-made textiles, on the other hand, where quotas became effective only recently, the comparison is between two future prices: (a) U.S. prices as they would be in a few years if quotas had not been introduced, and (b) the corresponding prices

---

[24] Department of Commerce, *Survey of Current Business,* July 1971, table 2.5. The figure is probably an understatement. In terms of weight, use of textiles for house furnishings amounted to 57 percent of the use for clothing in 1970. (Textile Economics Bureau, *Textile Organon,* November 1971, p. 161.)

[25] Ratios of cotton consumption to total consumption and of cotton imports to total imports in pounds are computed from tables in: Department of Commerce, Office of Textiles, Market Analysis Division, *Cotton, Wool, and Man-Made Fibers Manufactures,* March 1971. Ratio of the dollar value of cotton imports to the total value of textile imports is computed from *Cotton, Wool, and Man-Made Fiber Textiles, Tables Depicting United States Foreign Trade,* prepared by the same source, unpublished, March 1971.

as they will be after the quota effects have worked themselves out. Obviously, such a differential would be difficult to estimate even if the basic data on current prices were available.

As it is, the only available snippets of information on relative prices are estimates presented at congressional hearings by interested parties. Thus the National Retail Merchants Association estimated that quotas on non-cotton textiles "would cause a 15- to 25-percent increase in apparel prices." The American Retail Federation estimated the following retail price savings on "comparable key apparel items":

> Imported men's dress shirts save American consumers approximately 25 percent, imported boys' dress shirts 33⅓ percent, women's tailored blouses 33⅓ percent, imported women's walk shorts 37 percent, imported men's walk shorts 40 percent, imported men's ziplined raincoats 21 percent, imported women's raincoats 15 percent, imported acrylic sweaters 20, 30, and 33⅓ percent, and imported men's worsted wool suits 30 percent.

Price differentials are even larger in the view of a representative of importing firms.

> A full-fashioned long-sleeved ladies' sweater made in the United States would retail in our department stores at about $8 to $9. My firm has made the same garment in Taiwan to retail in this country at $4 to $5. A ladies' wool cardigan, full-fashioned, long-sleeved, produced domestically would retail at $11 to $13. The same quality sweater produced in Hong Kong sells at $6 to $7. [26]

The quoted differentials are between 25 and 100 percent of the non-quota price of the good. They occur, of course, in the most competitive imported goods. Other textiles that have not been imported even before quotas were introduced may be assumed to cost no more in the United States than imports would cost inclusive of tariff duties. The price differential of a large number of other textile goods must be somewhere between zero and the high figures mentioned above. The differential needed for the quota cost estimate is a weighted average of all the individual differentials.

Another piece of evidence may help in guessing what the average price differential may be. The actual pre-quota rate of increase of imports gives some indication of the comparative advantage of foreign producers. The dollar value of non-cotton imports was 70 percent

26 *Hearings*, May 20 and 21, 1970, pp. 1419, 1554.

higher in the first nine months of 1971 than in the corresponding 1970 period. The volume of these imports grew at a 77 percent annual rate from 1969 to mid-1971, while the domestic output advanced only slightly. The ratio of the volume of man-made imports to domestic consumption about doubled within one and a half years. An advance of imports as fast as this could not occur without a considerable price differential. The industry's estimate that import growth would spread, without quotas, to all categories of textiles and that within five years as much as 50 percent of the textiles consumed in the U.S. would be imported, although probably exaggerated, points in the same direction.[27]

When judging potential imports, the deterrent effects of a mere threat of quotas must also be taken into account. Foreign industry would certainly expand at a quicker pace if it did not have to base its plans on the expectation that growing sales will provoke protectionist measures.

From the above facts and considerations, I conclude that the average price of non-cotton textiles in 1972 will be at least 5 percent higher than it would have been without quotas. In a few more years, when foreign supply and thus imports would have increased further, it seems unlikely that domestic prices would be depressed by less than 10 percent. The calculations below are based on these very rough estimates, but the skeptical reader can easily substitute his own figures. It should be kept in mind, however, that a price differential of 10 percent does not have to mean a rise in prices by 10 percent. It can arise when prices remain constant under quotas while they would have declined without quotas, or it can signify a slight price rise with quota as opposed to a slight fall without quota.[28]

If the imposition of quotas raises prices by 5 percent or 10 percent, then abolishing the same quotas lowers them by about 4.8 percent or 9 percent. It will be assumed that this would be the effect of abolishing quotas on cotton imports since there seems to be no reason to expect the situation to differ in this respect from that of non-cottons.

---

[27] The import to consumption ratio for the fiscal year 1971 was computed from the Office of Textiles, *Cotton, Wool, and Man-Made Fibers Manufactures*, cited above and from unpublished tables prepared by the same source.

[28] The fact that quotas on woolen and man-made textiles cover at present (November 1971) only 57 percent of such imports in quantity terms and 53 percent in value terms, according to the Office of Textiles' estimates, can be disregarded for future effects. It can be safely assumed that quotas will be quickly imposed also on exports of other countries, just as cotton quotas covered at first only 10 countries and then spread to 27.

In evaluating the price differential the special influence of quotas on the composition of imports must be remembered. Because quotas limit the quantities rather than the values of imports, it is to the advantage of exporters to shift to relatively high-priced goods. It was noted above how Japanese exporters are forced to make such shifts for balance-of-payment reasons, among others.

The consequence of this shift is that imports of low-priced goods are cut far more than total imports. Sales of some goods will cease entirely and these tend to be goods which are not produced domestically either, even without imports. The consumer who is forced to switch to an entirely different commodity is likely to find that he has to spend several times as much as previously if he wants to obtain the pleasure he derived from the cheap imported good.

Such large margins, furthermore, occur not only in low-priced goods. Wherever a wide range of choice is an important factor in the satisfaction gained from an article, limitation of that choice is equivalent to a considerable price differential. A blouse or sweater which is "just what I wanted" because it was selected from a great variety of items has considerable more value than a "similar" article bought because it was the only kind available.

Results. With the help of the foregoing estimates of the price differential and the value of U.S. textile consumption, the tentative estimates of the cost of textiles quotas, given at the beginning of this section, can be derived. The calculation is shown in table 4 and a simplified account follows.

The $600 million loss suffered by users of cotton textiles in 1970 arises from an estimated 4.8 percent price differential on an expenditure of roughly $12,200 million. The loss of users of woolen and man-made textiles in the first year of quota limitations (1972) will amount, on the foregoing assumptions, to $1,900 million, which is 5 percent of the $38,500 million estimated expenditure on these goods. Assuming for simplicity that the cost of cotton quotas will not rise between 1970 and 1972, the total cost of textile quotas in the latter year may thus reach $2,500 million.

Allowing for the growth in the share of imports in textile consumption to be expected without quotas, the users' loss on cotton goods may, in a few years, amount to $1,100 million, or 9 percent of the basic expenditure of $12,200 million. Similarly, the loss on non-cotton goods may, by 1976, run to $3,700 million. This sum is a little less than 10 percent of the $38,500 million spent in 1970, because the price increase will cause a fall in the quantity consumed.

(A similar but smaller fall is taken into account also in the calculation for 1972.) The probable loss on all textiles thus comes to $4,800 million in 1976.

The estimates make no allowance for the upward trend in textile consumption, which rose by more than 50 percent (in pounds) in the decade of the 1960s. With population and income growing, further increases, although possibly at a slower rate, may be expected.

The total user costs of quotas, it will be remembered, consist of transfer costs, which are costs to consumers but gains to U.S. pro-

Table 4

ESTIMATED COST DUE TO U.S. IMPORT QUOTAS ON COTTON, WOOL, AND MAN-MADE TEXTILES, 1972 and 1976

Component of Cost	Unit	Symbol	Estimated Cost 1972	Estimated Cost 1976
(A) *Cotton*				
Consumption expenditure, 1970	$ billion	C	12.2	12.2
Price fall without quota	percent	p	4.8	9.0
Half of consumption rise without quota	$ billion	$\dfrac{c}{2}$	0.3	0.5
User cost	$ billion	$p\left(C + \dfrac{c}{2}\right)$	0.6	1.1
(B) *Wool and Man-Made*				
Consumption expenditure, 1970	$ billion	C	38.5	38.5
Price rise with quota	percent	p	5.0	10.0
Half of consumption fall with quota	$ billion	$\dfrac{c}{2}$	1.0	1.9
User cost	$ billion	$p\left(C - \dfrac{c}{2}\right)$	1.9	3.7
(A) + (B)				
User cost	$ billion		2.5	4.8

ducers, and national costs which are a pure loss to the nation. In view of the deficiencies of the data, no attempt will be made to estimate these component costs. However, it may be noted that the ratio of the national cost to the user cost will be larger, the larger the proportion of consumption that would be imported in the absence of a quota. Assuming, for example, that half the textiles consumed in the U.S. would be imported without quotas, then the national loss would amount to roughly one-half of the user cost.

Distribution of Burden

In evaluating the burden imposed by textile quotas, both its size and its distribution have to be considered. The burden falls most heavily on low-income groups and thus acts as a regressive tax. This fact stems not only from the general regressiveness of consumer taxes, but more importantly from special aspects of textile imports and quotas.

First, without quotas, a large part of textile imports would consist of the cheaper goods bought by low-income consumers. Hence, even if the import cuts affected all types of imported articles proportionally, a considerable quantity of inexpensive ones would be eliminated.

Secondly, the cuts are not proportional. They fall more heavily on low-priced than on high-priced goods because quotas cause exporters to shift into more expensive lines in order to take advantage of the limitations being set on the quantity rather than on the value of imports. The result is that low-income consumers will find that the goods they would have bought if imports were free are either more expensive or are simply not available under quotas. In the latter case a greater expenditure will be needed to provide the same degree of satisfaction.[29]

Technical Note: Alternative Estimate of the Cost of Textile Quotas

It may be useful to outline the findings of Andrew F. Brimmer's study of the cost of textile quotas (footnote 22) in order to permit comparison with the estimates of the present study.

At the time the Brimmer estimates were made, quotas on woolen and man-made textiles were being considered but were not in force. The study covers U.S. consumption of apparel of all fibers, that is, inclusive of cotton apparel already previously under quota. Textiles other than apparel are not covered.

---

[29] *Hearings,* May 14 and 18, 1970, p. 924.

The upshot of Brimmer's calculations is that the average price of apparel with quota limitations in force will, in 1975, be 3.5 percent higher than it would have been without quotas. The low price differential is derived in the following fashion:

First, unit values of imports and domestic production are calculated by dividing quantities in pounds into the respective dollar values. The unit value of apparel imports, adjusted to a retail basis, is found to have been about $6.10 in 1969. The corresponding value of domestic production was $10.30, or $4.20 above that of imports.

Next, the volume of imports that will be suppressed by the new quotas in 1975 is estimated at 430 millions of pounds or about 8 percent of U.S. consumption. It is then assumed that the price of these 430 millions of pounds will rise from $6.10 per pound, which they would have cost when imported, to $10.30 a pound which they cost when home-produced. The expenditure on these 430 millions of pounds thus would be higher by $1.8 billion under the quota than without it.

It is further assumed that apparel prices other than those of the suppresed imports are not affected by the quota. This means that prices of 86 percent of the apparel consumed which, on Brimmer's assumptions, is produced domestically with and without quota, remain unchanged and the same goes for imports entering under the quota (6 percent of consumption). On these assumptions the total increase in expenditure on apparel due to the quota would be $1.8 billion in 1975, a bare 3.5 percent of consumption estimated at $52.7 billion.

The assumptions, and hence the conclusions, on which the foregoing calculation rests are somewhat questionable, however. In the first place, the difference between the unit value of imports and the unit value of U.S. production cannot be interpreted as a difference between prices of identical goods. Two prices cannot prevail for a specific commodity in the same market. What the low unit value of imports signifies is that cheap goods have a large weight in the import commodity mix. In domestic production, on the other hand, goods with higher per pound value play a relatively large role. Therefore, the $4.20 differential between the two unit values measures the difference between the average prices of two different assortments of goods. There is no implication that the specific goods which are kept out by the quota will sell by $4.20 per pound more when home-produced. Nor does the comparison of the two unit values give any other clue about the effect of quotas on prices.

Secondly, it cannot be expected that most apparel prices will remain unaffected by a cut in imports. As the total quantities supplied at any given price are smaller without than with additional imports, prices of all competing goods must rise, rather than just the prices of the foregone imports. This means that the prices of the large amount of goods which would be produced domestically even without the quota and the prices of goods that would be imported under the quota cannot be assumed constant when imports decline.

Put differently, Brimmer's low estimate of the average price differential results from the assumption that prices of 92 percent of the apparel consumed will not be affected by the quotas. It is clear that even a large price increase confined to the remaining 8 percent of consumption cannot cause a large price differential for total consumption.

Since Brimmer's estimate covers only the rise in expenditure on those textiles which were imported without quota but are home-produced with the quota, it may be regarded as an estimate of production cost only, i.e., as excluding transfer cost, import cost, and consumption cost, as defined in our text. However, this interpretation conflicts with his statement that "the extra cost to consumers might be about $1.8 billion."[30] Also, the figure is too high if it is defined as a measure of production cost only.

---

[30] Brimmer, "Import Controls and Domestic Inflation," p. 3.

6
OTHER COMMODITIES

Dairy Products

Prices of dairy products, like those of some other agricultural commodities in the United States, are supported at levels above world prices. These high prices can be maintained because the Department of Agriculture stands ready to purchase the butter, cheese, and dry milk that the market will not absorb. An incentive is thus provided to foreign producers to sell such commodities in the U.S. market. If permitted, these imports could expand so much as to make the cost of the program of government purchase impracticably large. Therefore, in 1935, Section 22 was added to the Agriculture Adjustment Act of 1933, requiring the President, under appropriate circumstances and after consulting the Tariff Commission, to "impose such fees or quotas on the importation of the articles involved as he determines necessary." [1]

Mandatory import quotas on dairy products were first imposed under Section 22 in 1953. To the extent that those quotas conflicted with U.S. obligations under the GATT, such obligations were waived by a GATT decision of 1955. About a dozen articles were affected initially, but others were added during the following years. This action was taken as new products were designed by exporters abroad to avoid the quotas. For instance, import quotas were established on four products, effective January 1, 1971, three of which have never appeared in international trade until 1969. [2]

---

[1] U.S. Tariff Commission, *Quantitative Import Restrictions of the United States,* Publication 243, Washington, D. C., April 1968, pp. 18-20.

[2] Department of Agriculture, Trade Staff Committee, Report of the U.S. Government to the Contracting Parties on Action under Section 22 of the Agricultural Adjustment Act, Twenty-seventh Session, 1971, p. 26 (unpublished).

A few import quotas on dairy products are administered by the Bureau on a first-come, first-served basis; imports of all other dairy products under quota are subject to licensing procedures of the Department of Agriculture. The dairy products subject to such licensing procedures may be imported into the United States only by, or for the account of, a person or firm licensed by the Department of Agriculture, and only in accordance with the terms of the license. The license authorizes a particular firm to enter designated quantities of a specific dairy product from a designated country through a specified port of entry.

When issuing licenses the Department of Agriculture must, to the fullest extent practicable, assure (1) the equitable distribution of the respective quotas among importers or users; and (2) the allocation of shares of the respective quotas among supplying countries, based upon the proportion supplied by each country during a previous representative period, taking due account of any special factors that may have affected or may be affecting the trade in the articles concerned. In accordance with these directives, the department generally regards an importer who entered a dairy product during a base period as eligible for a license; he usually would be granted a share of the annual quota proportionate to his share of total imports of the product in the base period. Importers seeking to enter the trade may also be licensed to bring in nominal quantities of a single product. Licenses may not be transferred or assigned to others except as authorized by the Department of Agriculture.[3]

These complicated rules and laborious procedures have been set up to administer imports worth as little as $41 million in 1969, or only 0.7 percent of the value of U.S. output of dairy products. Similarly, in terms of weight, imports under the quota came to only 900 million pounds, which represented only 0.8 percent of the domestic dairy output (milk equivalent, fat-solids basis). Most of the licensed imports are cheese specialties.

Regarding the U.S. dairy industry, it may be noted that the volume of output in 1969 was the lowest since 1945. The value of this output, however, was the highest on record, viz., $6.2 billion. The volume of production of dairy goods reached a peak in 1964 and steadily declined thereafter despite the near complete protection.[4]

---

[3] U.S. Tariff Commission, *Certain Dairy Products*, Publication 338, Washington, D. C., September 1970, pp. A-14, A-15. The following data are from the same source and from these pages in the order given: A-28, A-1, A-13, A-55.

[4] U.S. Tariff Commission, *Certain Dairy Products*, Publication 340, Washington, D. C., October 1970, p. 105.

In addition to the imports within the control system, imports outside the system amounted to 700 million pounds in 1969, so that total imports of dairy products were 1.6 billion pounds, or 1.4 percent of domestic production.[5] Small as this percentage is, it is larger than those of the 1950s and early 1960s, which were only 0.4 to 0.7 percent. In 1966 foreign subsidies and consequent surpluses caused U.S. imports of articles not under quantitative limitation to increase suddenly so that the ratio tripled. Repeated extensions of the coverage of the quotas brought the ratio down to its present level.[6]

A fairly regular sequence of actions has developed in recent years: foreign exporters find it worthwhile to design new variants of dairy products to avoid existing controls, although they know that their quota avoidance will be of short duration. Imports of such new goods mount rapidly. The President orders an investigation by the Tariff Commission and, upon its recommendation, imposes quotas on the new products. The foreigners then design something different and the game continues.

In January 1969, for instance, the President imposed quotas on the products that had accounted for the bulk of the non-quota imports in the preceding 18 months.[7] But by 1970 the Tariff Commission had already found additional restrictions necessary for the four products whose history is shown clearly in table 5. The commission recommended zero quotas for the first three articles and a quota of 100,000 pounds—against imports of near 12 million pounds—for the fourth.

That exporters are willing to design new goods in order to escape the quotas for one or two years points to the large profit to be made from such trade. Indeed, the price differential is enormous. "For example, in March 1970 the wholesale price of butter (finest grade from New Zealand) in London—a principal market—was 32.1 cents per pound; in Chicago, it was 68 cents per pound. The price of nonfat dry milk in London was 9.4 cents per pound; the average U.S. market price was 27.0 cents per pound." The price-raising effect of quotas is often denied by their defenders. But in the case of dairy quotas high prices are openly upheld as one of the main purposes of the restrictions. Imports, however small, are blamed for causing U.S. market prices to be not as high as they would be otherwise.[8]

---

[5] TC Publication 338, p. A-55.

[6] TC Publication 340, p. 105.

[7] TC Publication 338, pp. 3, 4.

[8] Ibid., pp. A-21, 16, 17.

Table 5

U.S. IMPORTS OF SELECTED DAIRY PRODUCTS

(thousands of pounds)

Article	1963	1964	1965	1966	1967	1968	1969	Jan.-July 1970
Ice cream[a]	0	0	0	0	0	0	2,588	4,012
Certain chocolate and articles containing chocolate	0	0	0	0	0	0	477	7,156
Animal feeds containing milk or milk derivatives	0	0	0	0	24	2,399	9,693	13,650
Certain cheese and substitutes for cheese[b]	60	60	60	60	60	60	3,000	7,713

[a] Thousands of gallons.

[b] Estimated.

Source: Tariff Commission 238, p. 19.

The high extra expenditures imposed by dairy quotas on U.S. consumers of dairy products are probably for the most part payments for inefficiently allocated U.S. resources. Hence, they are a total loss to the nation. Another, probably smaller, part of the quota cost represents a gain to those domestic producers who could stay in business also if prices were lower. This is a transfer cost.

In view of the insignificant volume of imports, that part of the quota cost which is attributable to raised import prices (the import cost) must be very small. It is likely that these import profits are shared by the U.S. licensee and the foreign exporters' organizations.

As with other quotas, the distribution of the quota burden is regressive since consumption of dairy products is a larger item in low-income budgets than in high-income ones.

Meat

Meat import quotas are a good example of "voluntary" quotas: a sudden rise in imports causes the passage of a law which violates the principles of GATT and which, if enforced, would cause grave complications for U.S. international trade policy. The law is not applied but is enough of a threat to persuade meat exporters to sign "voluntary" agreements restricting their sales in the U.S. market.

Two years (1962 and 1963) of the "heavy" import of beef from Australia and New Zealand sufficed for the enactment of the Meat Import Law of 1964. "The legislation provides for the imposition of an absolute quota on fresh, chilled, or frozen beef, veal, mutton, and goat meat, if imports of these meats beyond specified quantities should be anticipated." These quantities are determined by the 1959-63 ratio of imports to domestic production of the types of meat covered, which amounted to 4.6 percent. Should, in the estimation of the Secretary of Agriculture, imports in the coming year exceed the amount which corresponds to this ratio by 10 percent or more (the trigger point) the President shall, by proclamation, impose quotas.[9]

In the period 1965-1967 imports were below the trigger point. However,

> in mid-1968 it became apparent that meat imports for calendar year 1968 would be large enough to trigger quotas under the Meat Import Law. But the United States was reluctant to impose quotas, if any other workable system would bring the desired results, because imposition of quotas would pose

---

[9] TC Publication 243, *Quantitative Import Restrictions*, pp. 54, 55.

the threat of retaliation from foreign countries against U.S. agricultural exports. So, in lieu of mandatory quotas the U.S. worked out arrangements with foreign meat exporting countries to limit their shipments "voluntarily" during the remainder of 1968 with the effect that Australia and New Zealand drastically cut exports to the U.S. already during the final quarter of the year.[10]

To date such "voluntary" arrangements have been renewed each year.

The distribution of quotas among the exporting countries is carried out by the Department of Agriculture. The task is particularly difficult because, on the one hand, Central American countries are not to be discouraged from increasing their beef sales, and, on the other hand, historical suppliers (Australia, New Zealand, Mexico, Ireland, and Canada) have been assured that their cooperation under the "voluntary" program would not impair their market shares.

The restricted imports consist mostly of chilled and frozen beef of a quality approximating U.S. cow beef. The bulk of this meat is used for manufacturing. It is processed into hamburger, sausages, TV dinners, and other products, and does not compete closely with the main type of U.S. beef production: steers and heifers for table use. Quantities of table beef imports are insignificant.[11]

The trend of table beef production and that of processing beef production move in opposite directions. Production of steer and heifer beef has nearly doubled in the U.S. between 1955 and 1970, rising from about seven billion pounds to about 13 billion pounds. On the other hand, production of cow and bull beef is on the downgrade and has, over the same period, fallen from roughly three and a half billion pounds to three billion.[12] This decline is due to developments in the dairy industry. Since 1950 milk cows on farms have declined by 34 percent, from about 22 million to slightly over 12.6 million in 1969. Meat imports thus can be regarded as replacing a product which is of dwindling interest to domestic producers.

Meat imports under the quota were 6.7 percent of total U.S. beef production in 1970, up from between 5 and 6 percent in the preceding decade. It may be more meaningful, however, to compare these

---

[10] U.S. Department of Agriculture, unpublished memorandum.

[11] Raymond A. Ioanes, "Current Developments in the World's Beef Industry," Remarks before the Annual Convention of the Oklahoma Cattlemen's Association, Tulsa, Oklahoma, December 4, 1970 (unpublished), p. 8. See also U.S. Tariff Commission, *Summaries of Trade and Tariff Information*, Publication 250, Washington, D. C., 1968, pp. 99, 111.

[12] Unless otherwise stated, all data are from unpublished tables of the Department of Agriculture. Where original data are given in pounds of carcass weight, I have converted them into pounds of product weight. The conversion factor is 1.3.

imports with the domestic production of beef for processing. On this basis, quota imports amounted, on the average, to 14 percent of domestic production in the years 1951-65 and to 17 percent in 1970.[13] The restrictive effect of the import policy becomes apparent when these percentages are considered in the light of the fact that U.S. demand and supply developments drove cow prices up by 37 percent during the 1960s, as compared to a mere 12 percent rise of choice steer prices.

There is no published estimate of the costs of meat quotas, so far as I know. An unpublished estimate by experts arrives at an annual cost of about $600 million. This estimate rests, first, on a finding that, for each 100 million pounds of additional imports following the lifting of controls, the average U.S. price of all meat would drop by 0.75 cents per pound and, second, on a finding that the total rise in meat imports due to abolishing the quotas would amount to 300 million pounds. The result is that the average price of all meat would fall by 2.25 cents per pound if the quotas were abolished. With total meat consumption in 1970 at roughly 27 billion pounds, the indicated annual saving in expenditure for meat approximates $600 million.

In this calculation the abolition of quotas would raise meat imports by 300 million pounds or 26 percent of present imports. This is 4 percent of the U.S. consumption of processed beef. The estimated increase is relatively small since a considerable part of potential imports would still be prohibited, namely, those from countries with foot-and-mouth disease. In particular, imports from Latin America would be excluded on this ground.

As to the price differential, it is important to note that the price of meat exported to the United States under the quotas is 10 to 20 percent higher than the price of meat exported to other countries.[14] Hence, one may expect the price of imported meat to fall by, say, 10 percent if quotas were abolished. This would cause a decline of similar magnitude in the prices of closely competing kinds of domestic meat and a much smaller decline in prices of those meats for which imports are no close substitutes. In this light the aforementioned 2¼ cents per pound decline (which equals about 2 percent of the current price) looks more nearly too low than too high.

---

[13] Calculated as the sum of (a) the output of cow and bull beef and (b) one quarter of the output of steer and heifer beef. The latter proportion is based on a Tariff Commission estimate of 1963 (TC Publication 128, June 1964).

[14] Council of Economic Advisers, *Economic Report of the President*, Washington, D. C., 1971, pp. 156, 157.

The higher price paid under the quota for imported meat goes to the foreign exporters since the quotas are allocated to them. However, due to the modest amounts imported, their profit is not large. The value of meat imported under the quota in 1970 was $580 million, reflecting an excess of, say, 10 percent over and above the import value at world market prices. Hence, this latter value would approximate $527 million and the corresponding profit would be $53 million.

Out of the aforementioned $600 million total estimated cost of meat quotas, $53 million thus would be accounted for by the extra profit of foreign exporters (the import cost). How much of the remaining $547 million is attributable to misallocated resources and how much to extra income of U.S. meat producers could be estimated only with calculations which go beyond the scope of this study. The same goes for an estimate of the consumers' loss incurred by switching from imported meats to other meats or other foods.

One thing is certain however: as is typical with quotas, it is the low price end of a class of goods which is being kept out and it is, therefore, the poorest consumer who pays most of the cost. Of beef consumed by households with incomes under $3,000, about 45 percent was of lower quality in 1965, while the corresponding percentage for households with incomes over $10,000 was only 23 percent.[15] The regressive impact of quotas is evident once more.

Petroleum

Oil import quotas are the costliest of U.S. import restrictions. They have also been studied more thoroughly than any other class of quotas, particularly by a cabinet task force as set forth in a report of 1970.[16]

First introduced as "voluntary" restraints in 1955, oil quotas were replaced within four years by mandatory quotas on crude oil and oil products. These quotas were based on provisions of the Trade Agreements Extension Act of 1955 and later acts authorizing restrictions on imports which would impair the national security. The provisions now in force are contained in Section 232 of the Trade Expansion Act of 1962. Although this section is not confined to the oil industry

---

[15] U.S. Department of Agriculture, *1965 Household Food Consumption Survey*, Washington, D. C.

[16] The Cabinet Task Force on Oil Import Control, *The Oil Import Question*, Washington, D. C., February 1970. Even more recent studies have been done for hearings of a joint economic subcommittee, January 1972. (See *Washington Post*, January 9, 1972, p. A-5.)

and, in fact, was invoked by other industries attempting to obtain similar protection, so far it has been applied only to the oil industry.[17]

The stated purpose has been protection of the national security, which requires "that we preserve, to the greatest extent possible a vigorous, healthy petroleum industry in the United States." [18] (Dependence upon a subsidy, in this view, is compatible with vigor and health.) In the words of the president of an oil company: "Dare we trust our future defense on the vagaries of global politics and the maintenance of supply through thousands of miles of submarine-infested waters?" [19]

Whether the import restrictions actually contribute to security is by no means clear, however. The policy may increase rather than reduce the necessity of imports in case of war. It is true that the high oil prices encourage exploration in the United States, but they also stimulate exploitation, and the net effect on U.S. reserves cannot be predicted.[20]

> The overall level of import restriction is set in percentage terms and has not varied significantly since the inception of the program. While there are numerous sub-categories within this overall limit, and some have been used to accommodate changing circumstances, no adjustment—except effective decontrol of residual fuel oil imports into the East Coast—has significantly altered the overall import level. Specific distinctions and adjustments are made for different regions and products.[21]

> Except for residual fuel oil, all unfinished oil and finished products imports are, in effect, carved out of the crude quota level. Thus there are two principal quota levels: the overall crude products quota and the residual fuel oil quota. Each of these varies geographically. . . . [East of the Rocky Mountains] the crude products level is set at 12.2 percent of estimated production.[22]

---

17 TC Publication 243, *Quantitative Import Restrictions*, pp. 50, 51.

18 U.S. Congress, Senate Committee on Finance, *Hearings on Import Quotas Legislation*, 90th Congress, 1st Session (1967), pp. 15-16, as quoted by Robert E. Baldwin, *Nontariff Distortions of International Trade* (Washington: The Brookings Institution, 1970), p. 38.

19 William H. Peterson, *The Question of Governmental Oil Import Restrictions* (Washington: American Enterprise Institute, 1959), p. 8.

20 Baldwin, *Nontariff Distortions*, p. 38.

21 Cabinet Task Force, *Oil Import Question*, pp. 8-10.

22 West of the Rocky Mountains (District V), "the crude-products quota is set at the difference between estimated demand for the calendar year and estimated U.S. and Canadian supplies produced in or shipped into District V" (Cabinet Task Force, *Oil Import Question*, p. 10).

Imports of residual fuel oil for use on the East Coast are effectively free of restrictions.

The result of the various limitations was that 23 percent of the oil consumed east of the Rocky Mountains in 1971 was imported.

"Imports are regulated by licenses issued by the Department of the Interior; allocations of the quota are made to individual companies, based principally on the amount of domestic crude oil processed in the preceding year."[23] The proportion of input that may be imported varies inversely with the size of the firm. In 1969 it declined from 20 percent for the smallest to 3 percent for the largest refiners.[24]

The allocation system thus discriminates arbitrarily among firms. It also entirely disregards the companies' previous foreign investments which were encouraged by the government to ensure access by the firms to low-cost foreign oil. With the introduction of quotas the value of such investments was reduced, however inadvertently. "On the other hand, to the inland refiner with no import history, the government's import license represents windfall profit."[25] The present import quotas thus have not only caused a shift from other industries into oil production, but also shifts within the industry.

However, the method used has a great advantage in comparison with those employed for sugar and textile quotas described earlier; the quota profit is not channelled to the foreign exporters but to the U.S. firms receiving the licenses. Thus the import cost of oil quotas is a transfer cost, whereas it is largely a national cost in the case of sugar and textile quotas.

The Cabinet Task Force on Oil Import Control reports that the domestic wellhead price of crude oil is $3.30 per barrel, compared to a world market price of about $2.00. The delivered price of domestic oil at East Coast ports is estimated at about $3.90, that of Middle Eastern oil including the tariff at $2.24 to $2.30.[26] Licenses—called quota tickets—are worth the difference between the domestic and the foreign price. The tickets can be traded. Inland refiners sell their allocations to coast refiners which use imported oil.[27]

U.S. consumers paid, of course, for the price differential. The Cabinet Task Force estimates the cost in 1969 at about $5 billion and states that, by 1980, the annual cost to consumers will approximate $8.4 billion. Other estimates are roughly of the same order. The

---

[23] TC Publication 243, *Quantitative Import Restrictions*, p. 51.

[24] Cabinet Task Force, *Oil Import Question*, p. 12.

[25] Peterson, *Oil Import Restrictions*, p. 52.

[26] Cabinet Task Force, *Oil Import Question*, p. 19.

[27] TC Publication 243, *Quantitative Import Restrictions*, p. 53.

task force does not give a complete breakdown of its "consumer cost" (our "user cost"). Production costs ("efficiency loss") are not estimated for 1969, but are expected to amount to $1.5 to $2.0 billion by 1980. These costs pay for the inefficient commitment of resources attracted to the industry by the artificially high price. They are national costs. The remainder, the largest part of user costs, are transfer costs that represent income channelled to the producing firms. By 1980 these will amount to $6.4 to $6.9 billion. The consumption cost (i.e., the cost due to foregone consumption) is not included in the Task Force estimate because so little is known "about the responsiveness to price reductions of demand for oil."[28]

The enormous costs and the inequities and inefficiencies of the present oil quotas persuaded the majority of the Cabinet Task Force to recommend their gradual replacement by an increase in the present tariffs in order to permit a slow expansion of imports. This proposal, however, was not accepted by the President. The task force claims that

> a tariff system makes imported crude and product supplies available to anyone willing to pay the tariff. It therefore frees domestic buyers . . . from strict dependence on particular suppliers. In addition, because a tariff would be designed to equalize domestic and delivered foreign crude prices, domestic producers would have a continuing economic incentive to reduce their costs so as to increase their market share. Tariffs hence stimulate internal competition— leading to greater efficiency—while rigid quotas tend to perpetuate institutional inefficiencies and fixed prices.
>
> No single aspect of the present system has engendered so much controversy as the allocation of valuable import rights among recipients. . . . The hazards of fallible judgment, combined with the ever-present risks of corruption, counsel strongly in favor of getting the government out of the allocation business as rapidly and as completely as possible. . . . A tariff system can have the advantage of reducing administrative costs and the danger of favoritism and corruption.[29]

Steel

In December 1968 the Japanese and certain European steel industries, accounting for about 82 percent of U.S. steel imports, announced their

---

[28] Cabinet Task Force, *Oil Import Question*, pp. 22-29.

[29] Ibid., pp. 87, 88. See also George A. Hay, "Import Controls on Foreign Oil: Tariff or Quota?" *American Economic Review*, September 1971, p. 688.

intention to limit their exports of steel mill products to the United States in 1969, 1970, and 1971.[30] The announcement came after a decade of sustained advance in steel imports, topped by a spectacular jump in 1968 that was largely provoked by anticipation of an August strike in the U.S. steel industry. Despite its emergency character this last event caused the pressure of U.S. steel producers for additional protection to mount, with the result that steel was one of the industries covered by the quota bills introduced in Congress in the fall of 1968. The bills were not adopted but to forestall their acceptance at a later date the Japanese and European steel industries offered to restrict their exports to the United States. After discussion with the State Department they undertook a three-year Voluntary Restraint Arrangement, an action which the chairmen of the House Committee on Ways and Means and the Senate Committee on Finance declared "a welcome and realistic step."[31]

The arguments in favor of limiting steel imports are, of course, similar to those encountered with any imported commodity, namely, that imports cost jobs and harm the balance-of-payments. But in addition the national security argument has also been cited in this case. A "healthy" steel industry, it is claimed, is a necessity in case of war. One may reply that it does not follow that about 15 percent of peacetime consumption is the maximum amount that can be safely imported.[32] Moreover, in the opinion of the Office of Emergency Preparedness, it does not appear likely that steel imports have reached such levels as to threaten the impairment of national security. Based on available information, the domestic steel capacity as a whole appears to be more than sufficient to meet emergency defense and essential civilian requirements.

The story of rising U.S. steel imports begins in 1959 when, due to the long steel strike, imports shot up from 1.7 million tons to 4.4 million tons, or from 2.9 percent to 6.1 percent of the U.S. market. From then on imports rose steadily, reaching 11.5 million tons or 12.2 percent of domestic consumption in 1967 and 18 million tons or 16.7 percent of consumption in 1968.

---

[30] In addition to the sources cited, various government memoranda and tables were used in this section.

[31] Chairmen of the House Committee on Ways and Means and the Senate Committee on Finance, "Release Letter from Secretary Rusk Announcing Voluntary Restraints by Japanese and European Steel Industries," January 14, 1969. See also Leonard W. Weiss, *Case Studies in American Industry*, 2nd ed. (John Wiley & Sons, Inc., 1971), p. 191, and Robert E. Baldwin, *Nontariff Distortions of International Trade* (Washington: The Brookings Institution, 1970), p. 34.

[32] Weiss, *American Industry*, p. 193.

Raw steel production in the United States also expanded vigorously in the 1960s. The rise was about 50 percent from 1959 to 1969, but most of it occurred in the first half of the decade. The growth of imports thus absorbed some of the increase in domestic consumption but was not accompanied by a decline in domestic production.[33]

Under the voluntary agreement the Japanese and Europeans were to limit their steel exports to the United States in 1969 to 5.75 million tons each, rising to 6.04 million tons in 1970 and 6.35 million tons in 1971. Including imports of non-rationed countries, total steel imports for 1969 were projected at 14 million tons or about 13.6 percent of U.S. consumption, a sharp drop from the 1968 figures given above.[34]

The early experience with these quotas was a rather unexpected one. It so happened that the initiation of the Voluntary Restraint Arrangement coincided with a sharp increase in world demand for steel. European shipments, therefore, did not even reach the agreed levels. Instead of the permitted 6 million tons in 1970, they amounted to only 4.6 million tons. Different was the case of Japan, however, where the quota was filled and the share of the U.S. Japanese steel exports fell nevertheless from 53 percent in 1968 to 35 percent in 1969.[35]

Even when "voluntary" quotas are not effective in reducing the quantities imported, they have far-reaching consequences for the economy. Of particular importance is the strengthening of monopolistic tendencies. In those exporting countries where the steel industry is not government owned, the quotas require organization of producers' cartels to administer the agreement and to allocate their shares to individual firms. This may conflict with foreign antitrust laws. On the U.S. side the agreement also may be inconsistent with antitrust policy. Moreover, international competition is especially important in a domestic industry as concentrated as steel.

A price differential to the disadvantage of U.S. importers appeared as soon as the institution of the quotas eliminated competition among exporters. This differential has consequences distinct from those flowing from the general rise in steel prices that followed the "voluntary" agreement.

---

[33] American Iron and Steel Institute, *Annual Statistical Reports.* Also U.S. Department of Commerce, Iron and Steel Industry Operations, Bureau of Domestic Commerce, February 1971 (unpublished tables).

[34] Joint Release of Chairmen, "Letter Announcing Voluntary Restraints."

[35] U.S. Congress, Committee on Ways and Means, *Hearings on Tariff and Trade Proposals*, 91st Congress, June 1, 1970. Statement of Dr. Joel B. Dirlam, p. 1880.

Steel prices rose in the United States in the first two years of the quotas by about 13 percent as against a total increase by 7 percent in the preceding nine years. Price advances of individual items were much more striking. For instance, the price of hot-rolled steel sheets rose from $88 a ton to $127 a ton between November 1968 and February 1969.[36] To what extent the import limitations contributed to these price movements is difficult to assess. Certainly other factors also played a great role. One was the increase in world demand, reflected in enormous rises in foreign steel prices; another was the end of the administrative intervention which had kept a lid on steel prices in the U.S.; a third was the rise in production costs, which, however, may have been facilitated by the import controls because producers were relieved of the pressure of foreign competition. But whatever the relative importance of the various causes of the advance of steel prices, one cannot deny the contribution of quotas to that advance.

The differential which developed between prices charged by exporting to American as opposed to other customers is a clear consequence of the quotas. For instance, the 1969-70 price of stainless steel coil from Japan rose in the U.S. from 38.5¢ to 54¢ per pound, while in Canada the price in 1970 was still only 42.6¢ per pound.[37] The price differential of 11.4¢ is the usual bonanza received by foreign exporters under "voluntary" quotas at the expense of domestic users of the goods.

Since steel is an intermediate good the immediate burden of higher prices is on the producers of steel-using goods. In many instances these are goods which compete with imported ones. Thus, a producer of stainless steel sinks complains that he cannot compete with his foreign rivals because he has to pay more for his raw material. Steel quotas therefore lead to demands for the protection of steel-using products.

Exports are affected in the same way by high steel prices. In 1968 "U.S. exports of products using significant amounts of steel totaled at a minimum $14 billion." If higher U.S. steel prices "raise the cost of our automobiles, construction, and electrical power apparatus and other manufactures of important export products, they may lose their advantage in crucial export markets. The perpetuation of the voluntary quota system . . . could spell the loss of exports far exceeding in dollar value the amount spent on imported steel even in

---

[36] Statement by Dirlam, *Hearings*, p. 1847.

[37] Statement of H. M. Weiss, president, Metal Masters of Baltimore, Md., *Hearings*, p. 1919.

1968."[38] More specifically, it has been estimated that "for every dollar's worth of steel kept out of the United States by import restrictions, over a half-dollar is spent on increased imports or reduced exports in other product lines because of the higher cost of steel inputs."[39]

Another typical effect of "voluntary" quotas could also be observed for steel quotas almost immediately after their introduction, namely, the shift in import composition toward high value products because of the fixing of quotas in terms of quantity. This shift occurred despite the promise of the Japanese and European signers of the agreements that they would "try to maintain approximately the same product mix and pattern of distribution as at present."[40] Imports of carbon steel, which is relatively low in value, fell while imports of steel products, which range in value per ton up to 10 times as high as carbon steel, showed an absolute rise.

So strong was the combined effect of the higher prices and the upgrading of imports that the total value of steel imports in 1970 was as high as in 1968 despite a more than 25 percent decline in volume over the two years.[41]

Needless to say, these effects on foreign trade are only a small part of the burden imposed by steel quotas on the U.S. economy. With steel sales amounting to around $20 billion, it is clear that even a small rise in prices involves considerable cost for the U.S. economy.

Other Products

Imports of raw cotton, wheat and peanuts are restricted by mandatory quotas of the same type as those in force for dairy products. These quotas are also imposed under Section 22 of the Agricultural Adjustment Act in support of the agricultural price maintenance program.[42]

Raw cotton. About 95 percent of the cotton grown in the United States is short-staple cotton. Since 1939 imports of this type of cotton have been virtually eliminated by the imposition of quotas. The total

[38] Statement by Dirlam, Hearings, pp. 1855-56.

[39] Gerald M. Lage, "The Impact of a Single Trade Restriction on the Balance of Trade," Workshop Series, TD 6924 (University of Wisconsin: Social Science Research Institute, May 1969), quoted from Robert E. Baldwin, Nontariff Distortions, p. 43.

[40] Joint Release of Chairmen, "Letter Announcing Voluntary Restraints."

[41] Weiss, American Industry, p. 193.

[42] TC Publication 243, Quantitative Import Restrictions: (a) cotton: pp. 23-28; (b) wheat: pp. 35-39, 126; (c) peanuts: pp. 39-42.

amount admitted is only 0.3 percent of U.S. production. But since part of the quota is allocated to China and India and has not been filled, actual imports are even less than quota allowances.

Ordinary long-staple cotton accounts only for around 5 percent of the total U.S. cotton crop. The import quota is equivalent to less than 2 percent of the domestic production of this class of cotton. Extra-long-staple cotton is the only kind for which sizable imports, relative to domestic output, are permitted. The quota is equal to the U.S. production of such cotton, which, however, represents only 1 percent of total U.S. cotton output. Short-staple cotton is allocated to countries on the basis of their sales to the U.S. in the 1930s. More than 60 percent is assigned to Mexico. Long-staple cotton quotas are global but are filled mainly by Egypt and Peru. The extra-long-staple cotton quota is sometimes filled on the day it is opened.

Roughly speaking, then, cotton quotas prohibit the import of raw cotton with only two exceptions: one being a small concession to Mexico and the other permitting the importation of a rare type of cotton.

Wheat. Mandatory quotas on wheat imports were instituted in 1941 and have not been changed, with minor exceptions, since that date. The quotas are part of a policy which supports the U.S. wheat price at a level above the world price.

Imports of wheat under the quotas amounted to about 1 percent of total consumption in the earlier years and to less in more recent years. Allocation is by country on an historical basis, with Canada's share being 99.4 percent. In short, apart from a modest concession to Canada, wheat imports into the United States are practically prohibited by quantitative limitation.

Peanuts. Imports of peanuts have been subject to quota restrictions since 1953. Here too the quota allowances are so small that imports make up only a fraction of domestic production. U.S. peanut prices are about twice as high as world market prices. Peanut quotas are global, but the main source of import is Mexico.

Other "voluntary" quotas. Very little information is available about "voluntary" restraints imposed by foreign exporters on their sales to the United States with respect to products not already mentioned. It is known, however, that this device plays a considerable role in the case of U.S. imports from Japan. Agreements limiting such imports "cover such products as tiles, bicycles, metal tableware, baseball gloves and mitts, umbrellas."[43] This list is not exhaustive. It has in fact been estimated that "in 1963 some 24 percent of Japan's exports to the United States were subject to 'voluntary' quotas."[44] It is likely that similar arrangements have been negotiated with other countries.

[43] Baldwin, *Nontariff Distortions*, p. 42.
[44] Leland B. Yeager and David G. Tuerck, *Trade Policy*, p. 5.